NCC
Saga

NCC
Saga

being a story of the LMS (Northern Counties Committee)
where the enginemen were the heroes
and the villain the diesel engine

R M ARNOLD

David & Charles : Newton Abbot

0 7153 5644 5

Set in IBM 11/13pt Press Roman
and printed in Great Britain
by W J Holman Limited Dawlish
for David & Charles (Holdings) Limited
South Devon House Newton Abbot Devon

Contents

List of Illustrations

7

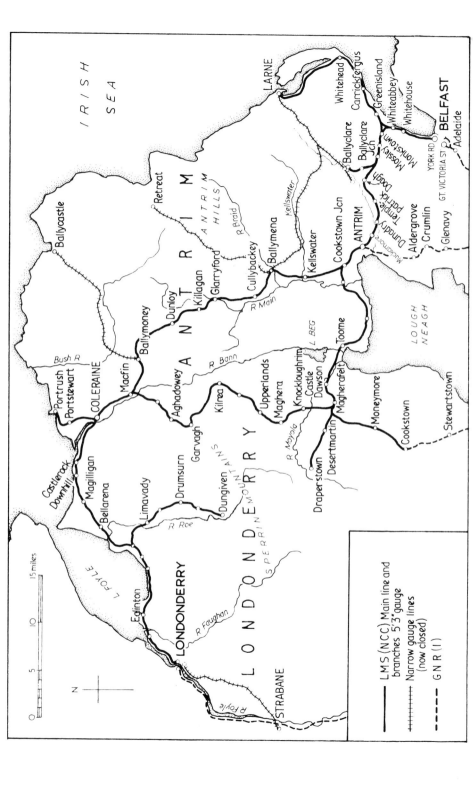

Preface

My own interest in the railway has very little of that which
compels one to try to run one's own, be it in model form or,
complete with appropriate uniform, in one of the preservation
societies. Nor, indeed, have I ever wanted overmuch to probe
into railway matters so ancient that no one alive has any
personal experience of them. Let us say, therefore, that I am
more a mere railway traveller, an observant passenger, almost
as curious today as to when, how and why the trains run as I
was forty years ago.

There does not seem to me to be anything very revolu-
tionary about this approach, but my previous book, *Steam
Over Belfast Lough*, has been described as an unusual book.
Certainly more Irish railwaymen than usual may have read it
for, as in this one, more prominence has been given to the
human element than usual, but those amongst them from the
NCC, never reluctant to call a spade a spade, have expressed
amazement and disappointment that I should 'waste time' on
BCDR matters, yet make no mention of the NCC main line.
So I have tried to rectify this by covering the remainder of
the broad gauge NCC as fully as is possible in the allotted
space. I had to decide between paring this or omitting various
statistical matter, the decision finally having to go against
those who enjoy studying logs of runs, locomotive and

carriage workings and shed allocations and rosterings. The author is aware that not every lover of the steam locomotive wants to be confronted with data concerning times and speeds. He feels, nevertheless, that the serious student of steam performance should be catered for, and the references to log tables are for such readers only, the tables appearing with other data about the locomotives, carriages and their workings in a separate supplement obtainable from the author at 57 Edward Road, Whitehead, Carrickfergus, Co. Antrim (50p) Useful dates and mechanical data about the individual engines also appear in the appendixes of *Steam Over Belfast Lough*, to repeat which here would be using up valuable space.

For the same reason I have not written a special chapter on performance, which must inevitably have made some kind of estimate as to how NCC locomotives stood in comparison with those of other Irish railways. In modern times there was frequent opportunity to compare NCC with GNR and those who were privileged to experience this will, no doubt, have made up their own minds as to whether the improvement in GNR performance, which coincided with an influx of NCC engines, had most to do with the engines themselves, a new generation of men on the footplate, or the management. Certainly on nonstop runs to Dublin the NCC locomotives wilted a little compared with large GNR 4-4-0s, especially with heavy loads, which is what one might expect for a mixed traffic 2-6-0 as against a large boilered passenger locomotive.

As far as NCC territory is concerned, individual performance of some seventy-five engines receives mention, over ninety per cent of those which appeared over the past thirty-five years.

CHAPTER 1

Main Lines

The broad-gauge NCC was neatly contained within two counties, if one disregards a couple of miles into Tyrone to reach
Cookstown. From Larne Harbour to Waterside Station in
Derry was 103½ miles and no two stations were farther apart
than these. One can understand Major Pope's fixation about
tank engines and strange it is that before 1946 so few were in
use.

But the authorities at York Road in the early thirties did
not regard their railway as a mere convenience for the
commuter, especially after they had gathered together a large
number of buses. Stations west of Cookstown Junction had
no facilities for a worker to arrive in Belfast before 9.15am
and in the evening it was even worse, for the last train to
Cookstown left York Road at 4.20pm. On the other hand
there were splendid facilities for Belfast folk to visit such
unlikely places as Killagan, Macfin and Bellarena. In 1939, up
to and including 12 noon, seven trains left Belfast for points
north of Ballymena. Two of these in addition threw off connections to Magherafelt etc but the corresponding number of
up trains arriving from the same points was but three, very
unusual when a railway's main station is also in an important
city.

The idea of the North Atlantic Express was a break away

from this tradition. It seems unlikely it was run especially for Sir Dawson Bates though no doubt his certain patronage was useful. The war then put paid to any opportunity of discovering if people were prepared to travel 65 miles every day to their place of business. Many were now forced to do so on account of the Blitz and other wartime circumstances and even the NCC now organised commuter facilities in a big way. When peace came this continued to be the new policy, although modern accountancy tries to prove its unprofitability, so maybe the NCC folk of the thirties were ahead of their time. Today there is no doubt that the government, who will have the last say, regard what is left of the NCC as serving little possible purpose other than keeping commuters' cars out of congested areas.

As far as express travel between its only two cities was concerned, prior to the building of the loopline at Bleach Green the NCC main line managed to travel in almost every direction of the compass, but even before that 2½ miles had been saved it was still 5¼ miles shorter than the rival Great Northern route to Derry. In 1939 the NCC's fastest Belfast-Derry train, the 6.20pm (there were several more only a few minutes slower), ran the 92¾ miles in 130 minutes with seven intermediate stops. Until the advent of the motorways this was a very reasonable challenge to the private car which had a road journey of only 74 miles, but the best the GNR could do (and a very smart train it was) was the 8.25am which required 155 minutes with the same number of stops. Before the war the amount of double track involved was almost identical between the two routes. For a dozen years after World War II the NCC steam-operated Derry trains maintained a steady 130-7 minute average for the expresses, though mainly at the even 2¼ hours. The best that postwar steam on the Great Northern could do was a timing of over 3 hours and even the advent of multiple unit diesel trains never produced a schedule nearly as fast as the NCC.

So most of the public, discerning or otherwise, travelled to and from Derry by the NCC. There is no doubt, however, that the GNR goods depot at Foyle Road was busier than the NCC one and this could not be completely accounted for by the fact that the Great Northern was involved with heavy cross-border traffic. By a curious progress of events this same traffic between Derry and Dublin etc is the only goods traffic handled by the modern NCC (now called Northern Ireland Railways), reaching Derry via Lisburn and Antrim since the GNR Portadown-Derry route was closed in 1965.

Let us introduce the reader to the NCC main line on a September day in 1947. We shall travel early, with the 8.25am express, because the intention is to visit Portrush first before going later to Derry. This is in keeping with NCC traditions. Partly because at one time the Londonderry and Coleraine Railway was a separate undertaking on the wrong side of the Bann, partly because 130 miles is a handy return trip, and partly because Derry hadn't at first a turntable large enough for the moguls, Belfast thinks of engines working to Portrush and back, and Derry of them working to Coleraine and back. Coleraine is neutral with troubles of her own in the shape of the Derry Central.

Our train will most probably have eight carriages, mainly composed of J6 and J12 corridor thirds but there should be at least one of the superb J4 centre corridor thirds (the best carriages in Ireland for the railway enthusiast), one of those interesting 1st/2nd side corridor compos with half compartment's and restaurant car No 88. This train, like the 5.25pm, invariably left from No 2 platform, though it was normal for the 9.25am Portrush train to use No 1 (the Larne platform). Each platform has destination indications on a winding roll, like the trams, and each departure an individual ticket checker at the separate barriers so the chance of joining the wrong train is very remote. Train arrivals, which are usually to the exact minute, are advised from the one signal cabin by ringing according to the platform number and all five platforms are suitable to receive trains.

Traditionally engines come onto their trains at almost the last minute at York Road. Some drivers like to approach with their engine at a long cut-off and brakes on to liven up the fire, but the Coleraine mogul for this job has been active most of the night, the fire having been cleaned after arrival at Belfast with the 2.45am goods ex Coleraine. As the train moves off there may not be a great deal of interest to view from an engine point of view, for at this peak hour of the morning all engines required will probably be busy elsewhere. However, just beyond the end of No 1 platform are the workshops and if the doors are open it may just be possible to catch sight of *84*, about to emerge from heavy repair, in the new and less ornate livery of black with vermilion stripe. It will probably not be quite possible to identify a mogul in the depths as *101*, in process of being reboilered and equipped for oil firing.

On the other side of the line, in the goods yard, the sight of *18* or *19* shunting would scarcely be inspiring to the English visitor but the more sharp-eyed may catch a glimpse of 0-4-0 tank *16* as she disappears across Duncrue Street into the dock area. The diesel shunter *17* may also be on view, possibly stationary, with a puzzled fitter standing alongside. On the same side, a little farther on, are the running shed, turntable and coaling plant and possibly a small audience to witness satisfactory departure of a crack train. Some cleaner may well decide to display knowledge and humour with frantic winding movements if Piggot or McDonald has his mogul too far out, whereas if our driver had been McClements the almost noiseless exit would be greeted mockingly with fingers in the ears of his audience.

For three miles the York Road station level is maintained at 17ft above sea level, the Cavehill mountain impressive on the down side, the Lough shore much less so on the other. About a ½ mile past the former station and block post of Greencastle, however, there begins the steepest mainline gradient in Ulster, which in 6 miles lifts us to an altitude of 339ft, higher than the line ever reaches again. The old route via Greenisland had nothing steeper than 1/89 but we have to climb 1/76 continuously for the 2½ miles from Bleach Green to Mossley.

But before this is Whitehouse halt in concrete, at 1/102, after which a cutting includes a short tunnel and ends at Whiteabbey station, followed by the junction at Bleach Green, with the Larne line dropping away from each side of this burrowing junction, unique in Ireland. Our mogul is now barking well on the famous viaduct. The curve on which wheel flanges react so threateningly in the other direction sharpens to a radius of 60 chains and we drop down our window to check the load, invariably finding both enginemen over on the driver's side, apparently doing the same. Now some concrete mileposts and three similar overbridges before Monkstown remind us that this stretch of railway is eighty-five years younger than that before Bleach Green. Between Monkstown and Mossley the slight difference in altitude with the original line is being gradually reduced. This is a stimulating piece of railway, the green fields which succeeded Valentine's Glen at the viaduct gradually giving way to a pine forest on the down side. From here the traffic by day in the lough several miles below is clearly visible, while at night the lights of County Down intermingle with the colour lights which guard Monkstown and Bleach Green junctions.

At Mossley the bank is at 1/89 and just before Ballyclare Junction station we have our first level crossing. Prior to the building of the loopline it was the fifth. Here are sidings on both sides of the line, that on the down side, 407 yards, being greatly the longer. The up grade eases further to 1/326 and two more level crossings, named Ballyclare Junction Nos 2 and 3, interrupt at minor roads before the summit at Kingsbog Junction, where the Ballyclare branch goes off on the up side, served by a goods train twice a week.

The busy main road makes a diagonal level crossing here, from which can be seen, beyond milepost 12, Ballyrobert Bridge, where was once a halt of the same name. Now our mogul is accelerating rapidly over reverse curves towards Doagh station, where the goods yard on the up side is rapidly beginning to share the postwar decline of three other small

stations before Antrim. As the line falls now at 1/178, it is
continually curving away from a wide valley below, where is
the village of Doagh. After Ballymartin crossing, at milepost
15, there is a long straight stretch, the gradient easing to
1/431 on both sides of Templepatrick station, the goods yard
of which, on the up side, saw during World War II as many as
40 wagons per day of bauxite loaded up from local mines.
Just over a mile farther is Kilmakee level crossing, comparatively quiet in 1947, the downhill steepening here to Dunadry
at 1/119. This station has also its station building and goods
yard on the up side and just beyond it we may catch a glimpse
of the Sixmilewater as we cross it on bridge 64, speed being
probably now at its maximum for the entire run.

Before Muckamore, where the York Street Flax Spinning
Company has sidings on the down side, the down grade has
eased to 1/298, after which a reverse curve is probably more
stimulating in the carriage than on the footplate, where at
least one sees it coming. The river is now far below us on the
down side and we race into a wide cutting, followed by the
rarely used Moylena crossing in an attractive wooded setting.
Here Antrim distant can be sighted and it takes good judgement on the part of the signalman there (and a knowledge of
drivers) to give a down train a clear road through without
undue delay to road traffic at the level crossing at the north
end of this station.

Though Antrim is a joint station, its NCC inheritance is
unmistakable. The major sidings with turntable and disused
engine shed are, however, on the down, or GNR side, there
being little on the other, apart from a few short sidings,
except the one time showground siding, later used by the
military. The down grade of 1/196 has eased to 1/1811 at the
station but now dips sharply for a short distance at 1/109 to
the foot of this ten mile bank. This is the lowest point of the
line for the next 32 miles,and just beyond is Springfarm
crossing, beside which goes off the 'Asylum' siding. It is a
favourite story on the NCC that a few inmates from the estab-
lishment situated at the end of this short, steeply graded line

Page 17   *(above)* Ballymena 1939. Class U1 *3 Glenaan*, constructed 1926 using parts of 'Light compound' 2–4–0 *33*; *(below)* Magherafelt, 2 August 1933. 'Light compound' *51* (rebuilt with '5ft' boiler) on turntable

Page 18 (above) York Road about 1920. 'Heavy compound' *34* Class A; (below) Draperstown, 5 July 1949. Class A1 4-4-0 *64 Trostan*

were once chatting to permanent way men working near the gate and asked them how much the railway was paying them. When told that the wages were a mere 12s (60p) per week the comment was 'It's youse boys should be in here, not us.' This siding is controlled from Cookstown Junction, two miles beyond Antrim, presumably because it can be entered only from the up line.

At milepost 23, on the down side, the remains of a platform suggest better days when a nearby racecourse was served by the railway. Here also is Niblock's level crossing, the line then curving round to cross over the main Ballymena road at Dunsilly. At Carngranny crossing the up grade at 1/326 steepens to 1/213 to Cookstown Junction, named Drumsough for at least the eight year period from 1848, when its present name would have made no sense. The present code letters, DS, perpetuate this in the same way as do CJ for Greenisland. The island platform, with the curious bay at the southern end , comes before the inevitable level crossing, at which the line to Randalstown goes off. Slightly the longer of two huge sidings here is that one on the down side called Shannonstown siding, 457 yards long.

After running level for a mile through Skegeneagh crossing to the one at milepost 26¾ called Aughleish, the line is now falling again, briefly at 1/142, and then more gently at 1/361 to milepost 28½. This is a boggy, rather unattractive area, though engrossing enough for the student of performance. The next crossing, Kellswater No 1, which crosses the line diagonally, resembles the two previous ones in that road requirements are so rare that it is normally set in favour of the trains. Yet another crossing, the tenth in nine miles, is at the north end of Kellswater station, where, like Doagh, the siding serving the goods yard can be served by up trains only. Now after a slight rise the line falls again to cross the Kellswater river at the point where it joins the Maine. This is the one hundredth bridge from Belfast and there now commences the long rise which, with occasional slight undulations, continues for 16 miles to a summit just before Dunloy. For 2 miles it is at 1/214 and it is this which provides the initial impetus for those splendid near mile-a-minute runs in the up direction. There is a hump after Slaght crossing and after the quiet but attractive Spencestown crossing we climb on a sharp curve past Ballymena goods cabin and block post, on the up side. The extensive goods yard is opposite on the up side and this was the extent of the original line of 1848.

The present magnificent station is a ½ mile farther, approached on an embankment after the fine stone viaduct over the river Braid. Built on an even grander style than Antrim, it was never a broad-gauge junction but seems even at the quietest period to have had at least four engines attached to its running shed, located beyond the north end of the up platform. Today *66* can be seen about to make a trip to the goods yard for a spell of shunting. There is also a line of derelict engines, including *13, 68, 71* and *87.* Although these are days when the future of many is uncertain, all these locomotives, with the exception of *68*, will be given a further extension of use, after overhaul. To reach the shed from the main line an engine has first to run onto the line on the other side of the up platform where once the narrow-gauge traffic was handled. At the north end of the down platform is a short bay, used to handle the perishable traffic.

The curve south of the station has required a speed restriction of 45mph and we start away on an up grade of 1/119, steepening almost immediately to 1/101. Soon a rock cutting gives way to a more pastoral setting near milepost 35. Here is Galgorm crossing, and Cullybackey is reached beyond two more crossings, a third being just to the north of the curving platforms. Beyond this on the down side is a goods shed with sidings and a 360yd relief siding. Had Kilrea been reached by building a branch from Cullybackey it could have been 12 miles nearer Belfast by rail than the Derry Central route.

Thence to Dunloy provides an interesting test of locomotive ability, as well as moments of attractive scenery. Broughdone crossing is on a 1/156 climb to Dromona siding, where a facing siding goes off to a creamery of that name. This was usually served in the early morning by the engine working the Ballymena-Cullybackey goods, but when shipping traffic offered an engine would go from Ballymena in the afternoon and this suited the various crossing keepers much better, for few drivers would refuse to carry one of these women into the town for a shopping expedition.

Approaching milepost 39 there is a fall at 1/133 to a delectable spot alongside the river Maine, though it is not actually crossed for more than two miles. From here the line rises at 1/117 round Dunminning curve, restricted to 60mph, and past Paul's accommodation crossing at a blind point for the pedestrian, so whistling is necessary. This sharp little hump is short but may cause the inexperienced timer, if he thinks the bank is persistent, to puzzle over his stopwatch reading.

Single since Ballymena, the line is level through Glarryford, which has a goods yard and a 350yd siding on the up side. Antrim and Ballymena had had water columns on both tracks, but the Glarryford one is now almost derelict, having never been very productive at the best of times. The next station, Killagan, also preceded by a level crossing, has the rest of its features similar to Glarryford and is approached up a 1/645 grade steepening to 1/329 beyond. Dipping down again at 1/191 to milepost 45, we reach the summit, less than a mile beyond, at 310 feet on an up grade of 1/204. Here are two crossings of the same name (Ballymacaldrick) and before Dunloy station is also a crossing and beyond, again on the up side, a 250yd siding.

Before the long fall to Ballymoney and beyond are two more quiet crossings near milepost 47, Goldanagh and Artiferral. Easy at first, the grade steepens to 1/149 at the double arch (milepost 48½). This goes under the main Belfast–Coleraine road and one can only assume that William Dargan, in plotting the route of this section (opened 1855), accepted a route two miles longer than the main road because anything more direct would have been too difficult. Certainly the Ballyboyland bank is quite tough enough as it is, and it is here at bridge 148 that firemen feel for the first time since leaving Portrush that they can relax a little.

Wonderfully varied in colour is the foliage of this part of the line and the acoustics too are remarkable. At milepost 49 one can hear a train leave Ballymoney 4½ miles away and then for a considerable time there is silence, though one is fully aware that the engine must be working hard. Ballyboyland quarry lies between two level crossings, Glenbough and Ballyboyland, and it depends upon the keepers concerned whether down trains surge across the two roads at 70mph or approach them whistling furiously. The grade past this quarry, which supplies the ballast for the whole of the NCC, is at 1/139, following a nasty little bit of 1/97. The siding, on the up side, is trailing for down trains and whilst blasting is in progress it is the responsibility of the Dunloy stationmaster to see that the tablet for the Dunloy–Ballymoney section is not issued.

Near milepost 51 the grade eases, but for a mile past post 52 it steepens to 1/114, gradually easing again to Ballymoney station. Here is still the subtle delight of two gauges and indeed *43* is at the head of the Ballycastle train in its bay across the up platform. All goods traffic is handled in the yard on the town or up side of the station and a Coleraine engine (*58*) can be seen making up a cattle special. Like the other passing points on the single line, the loop at Ballymoney is on the up side, but as it has the station exit and buildings, drivers have usually to endure the more cautious approach involved in running into the up platform, unless of course two trains are crossing. In the case of our 8.25am and the 8.30am ex Derry the latter, due one minute after us, uses the up platform. In such circumstances when the down train arrives first an apparatus near the water column at the north end of the down platform can deliver the Ballymoney–Macfin tablet after the arrival of the up train, thus saving someone a long walk from the cabin at the other end. Portstewart had a similar arrangement, but at Dunloy, with a long train, the signalman could be seen bumping along the trackside on his motorbike.

We are not affected by a speed restriction of 45mph over the curve at the north end of the station, but on this short uphill section it is rather tempting for drivers of nonstop trains. However, from milepost 54 it is downhill, easing from the 1/142 before Caldagh crossing to a longer stretch of only 1/1186 through Balnamore. We can now take in our stride a sharply upward approach at 1/109 to Macfin, where the Derry Central branch trails in on the down side. Before the war, because of the limited size of Macfin loop, the Portrush Flyer (7.10pm ex Portrush) was instructed to run forward to a stop in the DC branch, if loaded to more than nine bogies. This was so that the booked crossing with the 6.20pm ex Belfast would not be impeded. Nothing was left to chance in the planning in those days, though one might pause to reflect just how often the 6.20pm itself would have been too long to use the loop.

Macfin hump finishes with a little downhill at 1/142, followed by a short upward stretch, gratefully received by up trains, with so much adverse travel ahead. After Damhead crossing and the 'two-mile' bridge there is more downhill at 1/142 before we pass under the Lodge bridge, with Coleraine colour-light signals in sight. This important junction is approached on a curve, with the goods yard and extensive sidings on the down side and Henry's siding on the other, from which engines can reach the two-road shed. Six engines could be accommodated here, as long as there was only one mogul in each road.

The so-called 'fast' road through Coleraine is the up line. across the platform of which is a bay used by most Derry Central trains. The down platform has the ticket barrier and most of the business, but for the most important mainline station outside Belfast it is a miserable building and a great pity that none of the plans to rebuild it have been implemented. A 2-6-4 tank seems unusual to be taking our Derry portion forward but *1* and *8* can both be seen now regularly on mainline duties, the former shedded at Belfast in charge of W.R. Wilson and James Keenan. The only other engine to be seen is *64*, which has presumably worked the 6.40am ex Derry.

Our train to Portrush will be the last two (or possibly three) of the carriages which left Belfast. We pass over the busy station level crossing and take neither the first line to the left (which leads to Coleraine harbour) nor the second, which goes to Derry. After Calf Lane crossing, a ¼ mile down the Portrush branch, we commence a 2½ mile climb which could frequently be accomplished more easily by a through train if Coleraine's signalling system permitted faster through running. The line rises at 1/139 past a pretty accommodation crossing (to a well sited cemetery) and up under the Shell Hill bridge, popular each May during the North-West motor-cycle races. After easing to 1/193 the line then steepens to 1/121 before passing under Dundooan bridge. The summit is just after the next, the Black, bridge and Portstewart is approached downhill at 1/202. A level crossing precedes this crossing station, the up platform of which has been lengthened in concrete. Here is a small siding beside a water column at the end of the down platform, formerly powered, like a few other NCC columns, by a windmill. There is a bus connection here for the 1¾ mile run into Portstewart town.

The extremely marshy tendency of the station area gives way to rocky terrain as we climb at 1/187 until, for the first time for 57 miles, we can again see the sea, but now it is the Atlantic Ocean. After milepost 66 and Craigtown Bog crossing the line drops quickly into Portrush, first at 1/122 and then, past Glenmanus stone siding, at 1/76. A high embankment above a popular stretch of sand brings the line well into the town at road level, 55ft above sea level. On the up side, rather near the edge of the embankment, is the turntable.

The signal cabin is at the end of the original platform (No 1) but this train will normally use No 2, across the platform of which is No 3. With various sidings available, including the harbour tramway, and run-round facilities laid from all three platforms (sometimes even the run-round roads had to be used as sidings), Portrush, though better equipped than any other seaside terminus in the north, required careful planning on a busy day. I have a note of departures after 5.30pm on 15 July 1936 and this intensity of traffic was still not uncommon in 1947. Locals to Coleraine left that day at 5.45pm, 6.40pm and 7.30pm, and to Ballymoney at 9.15pm. Belfast trains left at 6.10pm, 7.15pm, 7.25pm, 7.40pm, 7.50pm, 8.00pm, 8.30pm, 8.40pm and 8.50pm. This entailed over 600 miles of travel for the engines concerned that evening, probably unique in Ireland.

We are back at Coleraine station, a tremendous focus of activities during the war and still the nerve centre of the NCC. It is not so long since the 'Tabernacle', a peacetime caravan coach lying in the bay across from the down platform, provided hospitality for enginemen from all parts of the NCC. When, just before the commencement of a run out of Derry with the daily leave train, Dan McAteer partook too liberally of a bottle of gin offered him by a USA serviceman, his fireman, who as a result was forced to assume all footplate activities from Eglinton forward, gratefully accepted help at Coleraine to carry the unconscious driver inside and away from prying eyes. But by 1947 lodging turns have ceased and many of the old characters have retired (in some cases not a minute too soon). Gradually the old engines too are being replaced and *8* is a case in point, for Derry and Coleraine men are having quite a job getting her to steam. Various little remedies, such as rings in the blastpipe and 'steam guns' to clean the tubes, have not yet been applied.

So we await the 11.55am to Derry, which is the boat train from Larne Harbour. Like every other country NCC shed, the Coleraine one is easily observed from the platforms and *83* is there in steam. In the area behind, the roof of a football stand reveals the presence of Coleraine Show Grounds. It is traditional here, when Coleraine has a home game, for the railwaymen to use convenient carriage roofs to observe the play. If none are suitably placed judicious shunting can no doubt remedy the situation, but Sam McNeill, the carriage examiner, is independent of this, the best signal steps being his private reserve. Just before our train of five bogies and a couple of brown vans departs with *64* the 11.5am ex Derry arrives, headed by *4A*.

The 33½ miles to Derry are very remarkable in that as soon as we have crossed the Bann, a ½ mile away, the entire line rises higher than 20ft above sea level only once, and that momentarily only for the Castlerock tunnels. Another unusual feature of this railway is that after bridge 191, near milepost 63, there is not one overbridge, apart, of course, from the Castlerock area, for over 32 miles. Indeed, apart from the estuaries of the Roe and Faughan the only obstacles are a few drains and mountain streams, averaging less than one per mile, compared to the Belfast-Coleraine line, with 187 bridges in less than 62 miles.

So we cross the Bann by the 1924 bridge, farther down the river than the 1860 construction, part of the line to which has survived as the Harbour branch. No wonder it was considered apt to name an important engine after this river, the largest in Northern Ireland, up which the Vikings had sailed. Even the Ballycarry poet, John MacNeill, felt constrained to write a poem about 'The Bann'. Though it was primarily intended to commemorate driver William Semple of Larne shed and Magheramorne it is no mean effort as locomotive poems go. Apart from the bridge at Coleraine the NCC crosses the Bann at two other points so its association with this river is stronger than with any other. Upon reaching Grangemore crossing near milepost 65, the curves of the riverside section straighten out as we run through sandhills towards Barnmouth crossing, where there is, at suitable seasons, probably the best floral display at any crossing on the NCC.

Castlerock, whose modest delights the NCC has tried to publicise with a cheap fare policy, has two curving platforms after its level crossing, the fortieth of some fifty gated crossings between Belfast and Derry. The summit of the line, at 55ft, is reached on a 1/120 gradient just before the station, alongside its small goods yard. Through the station the line falls at 1/545, sharpening in the tunnel to 1/279 until, after

Downhill, we are only fractionally above the wonderful long Strand. From the siding at the west end of Castlerock station, used nowadays mainly for caravan coaches, can be seen the mouth of the first tunnel and above it the famous Mussenden temple. One is tempted to wonder what that Bishop of Derry would have thought of the NCC and if he might have been prepared to perpetuate some of its steam engines in the same bountiful and striking way that he did for Anna. The short stretch of open between the two tunnels (page 69), cut out of that mighty basalt cliff, has an awesome character of its own, and one should remember that the contractors of the Londonderry and Coleraine Railway were tackling this impressive piece of railway construction before even the Belfast-Ballymena section was completed.

Downhill's single platform on the down side is preceded by a small siding, also for caravan coaches. Above are more towering cliffs with waterfalls and below a great abundance of fine dry sand, so much so that periodically Coleraine had to send out an engine and wagons on a Sunday to clear it off the track. Among the sandhills is 'Butchers' crossing and then, diagonally across the main road, Umbra level crossing. A short distance beyond is Heard's accommodation crossing, and then round the bend, Woodtown crossing, little used.

Afterwards there are only two points where the road to Limavady comes remotely near the railway and there is a station at each. Magilligan's building in typically red brick is on the up side, as is a short siding before the station level crossing. Further roads leading up the pretty, hilly area result in level crossings at Duncrun (Lower and Upper), preceded by Clooney. Bellarena is a block post and has a level crossing and even a water column. After this the line is rather remote from habitation for the remainder of the run to Derry, none of the stations being near townships. In fact one can often see at Bellarena cans of drinking water being placed in the guard's van for use of folk at Limavady Junction and Eglinton, where there is no supply.

After Carrowreagh crossing is the Roe bridge, from which

the line curves sharply round to run due south through more crossings at Oysterville and Myroe before a 25mph restriction introduces the curving platforms of Limavady Junction. The branch tails in on the other side of the down platform so here at least the NCC can produce a more recognisable branch train scene, with *70* on the job today. It was on such an occasion that that inveterate student of his fellow drivers, Billy McDonald, could have been observed calling over fireman Dunlop to witness Jimmy Logue's departure with a mainline train. As Logue struggled frantically with the 'Whippet' regulator two smiling faces expressed a little contempt for any driver who did not seem to know that all he had to do was to notch up and the regulator would move freely.

Since Downhill the line has been almost entirely at 18ft above sea level. This is typical of the reclaimed treeless area of flat lands which stretch northwards in the direction of Innishowen Head in County Donegal and contrasts sharply with the 1260ft high Benevenagh, dominant on the other side of the line. The trailing siding before Ballykelly airfield is on the down side. During the wartime construction of this aerodrome, workmen's trains were run from Derry and stopped at a point known as Drennan's Farm crossing to save them the walk from either Ballykelly or Limavady Junction. On the inland side are the platform of Ballykelly and Carrichue and also the latter's trailing siding. The line continues past Faughanvale (a short-lived early station) fringing a somewhat desolate shore, attractive only to bird-lovers.

Now, on the down side, comes the considerable expanse of Eglinton airfield, the building of which, during World War II, required a temporary platform at Longfield for the use of a large number of workers, mainly from Derry. At Donnybrewer is the first level crossing for seven miles and a siding here was invaluable to help handle heavy wartime traffic at Eglinton station. The level crossing at the latter is just beyond the platforms, the down one of which is very short.

Lock crossing at bridge 219 is the only point of note before we reach the bridge over the Faughan. On the other side a siding comes in from Coolkeeragh brickworks, followed immediately on the same (down) side by the platform of Culmore station. Level crossings precede Lisahally, where during World War II seagoing activities were so great at this narrow point of the Foyle that for a time a shuttle rail service was run between there and Derry, after a 270yd loop had been constructed, with signal cabin at its Derry end. Already in 1947 the wartime sight of dozens of ships, of various types, has greatly declined, and the passenger platform on the up side is no longer in use. It is now even quieter than in the pre-war days when a Pinkerton box controlled a siding down to 'the hole', which was all Lisahally implied.

For the last four miles into Derry the line at last becomes scenic again. The Lough is widening out and after Gransha crossing at milepost 93 the picturesque sweep of Rosses Bay ends in a sharp curve as Waterside station is approached, with a very fine view of the western side of the city across the Foyle and Derry harbour. The extremely cramped site of the goods yard is between the station and the river. Before the Cookstown Junction turntable was brought to a site on the down side of the track at Derry, large engines tended to obstruct the running line in the turntable's original position on the riverside, so its movement was controlled from the cabin. At the city end of the goods yard a gate indicates the extension onto the harbour tramway. Nothing larger than a 'Whippet' is permitted to shunt beyond this point, the Harbour Commission tank engine coming across the lower deck of the Craigavon bridge to collect any wagons. During the summer of 1972, some ten years after the dock lines had ceased to function, the surviving dock engine *3 R. H. Smyth* became the property of the RPSI at Whitehead, presented by Rev L.H. Campbell of Portstewart.

The two-platformed station at Waterside has a rather more spick-and-span appearance than Derry's equally interesting GNR station just across the river. The NCC always gave generous excursion facilities from Derry to seaside stations such as Castlerock and Portrush. Doubtless they were taking into account equally cheap trips to Bundoran on the GNR. Waterside seemed to rank higher than any NCC station in the life of the community and there has invariably been a lively selection of folk on the platform to bid goodbye to important trains. Presumably these were often Donegal folk, passengers on the train being friends on the first stage of return to a job in Britain or even emigration.

Possibly because of the existence of accommodation for taxis and mail vans alongside, No 2 platform, on the down side, is most used (page 70). At the engine shed beside the end of this platform *8* and *82* can be seen as we arrive, the former for the 1.20pm Belfast train. In 1938 this shed had six engines, usually all 'Whippets', a Derry engine working into Portrush every day. These small 4-4-0s handled almost all trains over the section to Coleraine. Even as late in time as 28 November 1945 I observed *33* on the heavy 2.20pm boat train to Larne Harbour (as far as Coleraine) and other 4-4-0s noted in the Derry area the same day were *1, 24, 50, 69* and *71*.

Many tales are told of the enginemen at Waterside shed. One concerns the cleaners, who had the moral responsibility of wakening Jimmy Logue to catch the first train to Limavady each morning. This old driver appears to have had a curious preference for the men's 'torry to that of his own bed at home. One morning a young recruit was handed a bundle of waste (which contained a detonator) to throw into the fire-box of one of the engines on his way to arouse Logue. Unaware of what he had done, the lad was just looking through the window to make sure that the driver was indeed awake when there was a violent explosion. No doubt the startled old man thought his last hour had come and the white face staring through the window can scarcely have helped. Since 1968, of course, both young and old in Derry have become more attuned to explosive noises.

CHAPTER 2

The Branch Lines

The previous chapter was concerned with some hundred miles of the NCC over which there is still a reasonably frequent passenger service today, though, of course, no steam operations remain. Most of the remainder of the broad gauge, however, barely survived into the main period of this book.

LIMAVADY AND DUNGIVEN

As was obvious from the facing points at Limavady Junction (Broharris) the Londonderry and Coleraine Railway of 1852 ran into Limavady direct from Derry. From the 79¾ post of the junction platform it was 3¼ miles to the town. But first, a ¾ mile away, was Broighter Halt, a single platform on the down side before crossing gates, and not greatly patronised, except by school children. Still almost level the line then passed under a road bridge known as Scott's arch, curving past a wooded estate (known locally as Ogilvie's plant'in) and across the river Roe into a good central position in the town.

For the extension to Dungiven a route a little east of the fringe of hills was used instead of the river valley. At milepost 84 (from Belfast via Greenisland) the slightly upward tendency sharpened to 1/90 and for the next 5½ miles to the summit there was nothing easier, 1/73 stiffening to 1/70 just before Ardmore station (85¼ miles). This was the least important of the line's intermediate stations and during the last years the goods was not booked to stop, though it usually did. From its platform on the line's up side, Balteagh church could be clearly seen to the east, the road to it and the nearby cross-roads passing under the railway at the station.

For the next mile the climb was at 1/72, easing considerably then through a level crossing into Drumsurn (88¼ miles), the village of this name lying to the east. With platform and siding on the down side, this was the most important station. The summit point beyond was at an altitude of 310ft so the line had risen 290ft in 7 miles. The steepest part of the line now followed, with just over a mile downhill at 1/69. The river Gelvin was crossed on a high bridge, after which an embankment was followed by a bridge over the road and, a ¼ mile farther, Derryork station (90½ miles), like all others on the branch the familiar red brick. Here facing points from the Dungiven end produced a siding against the gable of the station house. The 1535ft of Ben Braddagh looms up quite close to the east. This mountain and Craiggore, farther north, were considered by H. P. Stewart when selecting names for the A1 class 4-4-0s but *63*, which was to have been Ben Braddagh, was instead built into a U2, as was *59*.

For the last 2¾ miles to Dungiven (93¼ miles) the line resumed its upward tendency for a mile at 1/94 and then undulated a little before terminating at a point 273ft above sea level. From the station one had to descend to a bridge over the Roe to reach the main part of the town. A single platform on the up side had a run-round for the engine and a line through the goods shed to the loading bank, from which another line connected to the run-round. A square red staff controlled the branch and opened Derryork and Drumsurn sidings. The usual procedure, as it suited the sidings, was for the goods to serve intermediately en route to Dungiven, then run back nonstop to Limavady. In the mid-thirties the 10.40am goods ran the 10¼ miles in 27min, brisk indeed for a 15mph branch, on which the restriction was later raised to 25mph, though the schedule at the closure was 35min. Bob

Young, who was lame, officiated at Drumsurn, and here and on the others also a few buckets about the platform might find themselves filled with coal, the crew in turn benefiting by a pound of butter or some eggs, which can be boiled to perfection above the firebox.

As befitted an important town, the layout at Limavady was quite substantial, but confined to the area between the Roe and the bridge at the south end of the station where Main Street crossed over the line. The long low station building in the inevitable red brick (as was the station-master's house behind it) adjoined a single platform on the up side of the line. Many a fireman, at the right season, had nipped round for an apple from the orchard of stationmaster Woods. Against this the atmosphere at times was one of intense discipline, with 'ticket collector' Robinson, whistle in mouth, indicating thus to the driver the exact point at which he should stop. This performance so enraged Coleraine driver Johnny McAuley (reared in Limavady) that eventually he stepped off his engine to assure Robinson, in his best falsetto, that he knew more about this station and indeed the town than that worthy ever could.

To run round, an engine had to pass under the town bridge and then back past the loading bank, this line forming a siding which continued past Semple's yard to a stop block at the river edge. From this spur the quite considerable yard could be shunted, on the Benevenagh side of which was the derelict engine shed, still housing two engines in the late twenties. 2-4-0s seem to have been the dominant type including old *4* (scrapped in 1905) with tall chimney and tender cab, *12* and *14*, and later, *41*, again with weather protection.

The only trackwork on the up side of the station led to the cattle dock, to enter which the tablet was necessary. It was during heavy shunting here one day that Sammy Mills asked his young fireman to keep a sharp lookout from his side. As the engine pushed a long rake of wagons towards the stop block the stationmaster, who was assisting with the shunting, gave the standard sign with his hand for rapid deceleration, whereupon the lad remarked across the footplate to his driver, 'That stationmaster is a very nice man. He keeps waving to me.' The impact a few moments later almost demolished the last wagon.

The deterioration in status of the stationmaster is regrettable. In modern times, if there was one at all he was either a figurehead for walking about the platforms, as at York Road, or else a fairly abrupt booking clerk, none too pleased at being disturbed. But here at Limavady, apart from traffic involvement, the man was responsible for quite a large staff (four clerks in the goods office, for instance.) Sometimes it was necessary to adopt a moral tone. He had on one occasion to interview one of the men to advise him that he had been selected by a local girl as the cause of her (increasingly obvious) condition. The accused man stood in gloomy silence for a time before producing this gem of male philosophy: 'It's a fault, Sir, if you do, and it's a fault if you don't.'

Any class of engine, including moguls, was permitted as far as Limavady, though 'Whippets' were supposed to be the largest type allowed to proceed to Dungiven. However, it seems clear that 'Castles' occasionally breathed the Dungiven air and if some genius had sought to question this there was the remarkable information in the working timetable that the maximum load for a mogul or a 2-6-4 tank between Limavady and Dungiven was 360 tons. In 1936 Derry shed had the entire responsibility for the working of the branch and page 87 shows that even as late as 1949 driver Faulkner (that ardent footballer) of Derry had *58* (a Coleraine engine) at Dungiven with the daily goods. From this time forward she was easily the most regular performer on the branch, her tender having a fitting for weather protection.

In 1936 the day began with the 7.10am passenger ex Derry, which stopped everywhere to Limavady Junction. Here wagons detached from the 6am goods ex Coleraine were added before proceeding into Limavady. After some shunting a passenger train was worked to the junction at 9.5am, returning at 9.22am. This had the same set which had come from

Page 35   *(above)* York Road station, Belfast, 17 July 1937. Class U *73* shortly before rebuilding to Class U2; *(below)* Driver John Boyd at York Road about 1924, Class B1 4-4-0

Page 36   *(above)* Antrim, 1956. Driver Jock Orr of Ballymena with
Earl of Ulster; (below) York Road, 1933. Class D1 *Jubilee*
after working boat express from Larne Harbour during railway
strike. White-collared staff in charge during emergency:
J.H. Houston (driver) and J.D. McKelvey (guard)

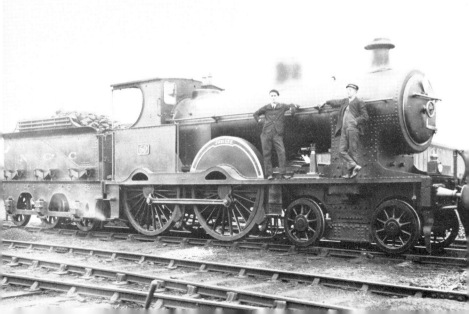

Derry, two old bogies (one third and one compo) and a four-wheeled guard's van. The engine then set off for Dungiven with the goods, so a bus (even at that period) provided a connection over to the junction for the 9.55am Derry-Portrush.

Further trips to the junction were made by this engine and set at 12 noon, 6.2pm and 8.9pm, a fresh Derry crew being obtained when the engine worked the 12.30pm goods ex Limavady and then the 3.5pm passenger Derry-Limavady, for the little passenger set had been attached to the goods. Engine and carriages returned to Derry with the 8.50pm goods ex Limavady.

Three years later a change of policy, which was to last till the branch closed, saw Derry fade in importance. There was now a 6am goods from Coleraine to Limavady and, as this engine now worked to Dungiven, it left Coleraine tender first, just in case the load was more than the usual dozen wagons and sanding had to be resorted to on the banks. Thus there was now an engine available in time to work a train to the junction at 8.23am, this connection into the 8.5am ex Derry being previously provided by a bus. The 9.5pm goods back to Coleraine (postwar 7.20pm) could at times be as heavy as sixty wagons, 58 sometimes providing a nasty experience for her crew by falling to walking pace through Downhill tunnel.

The shunter at Limavady was William Bond, a very large man who was never to be seen riding on the engine's steps as so many do. William kept himself to himself and walked every yard. As far as the branch train was concerned it was a great nuisance to have to couple and uncouple the engine so often every day so eventually a guard's van was provided with additional lookout facilities at the Limavady end, the engine simply propelling the train from the junction to Limavady on each occasion.

Passenger trains to Dungiven since 1933 were few, and due almost entirely to Bank Holiday excursions in peacetime and movements of troops during the war. For example, arrangements for 3 August 1936 show an empty train of thirteen six-wheelers leaving Coleraine at 5.30am, part of this going forward from Limavady to Dungiven at 7.40am to form a 8.25am excursion, which did not proceed forward from Limavady to Portrush till 9.20am. If at all possible Coleraine liked to hold on to a V class 0-6-0 for this job.

During World War II Limavady was one of three petrol depots for the military in Northern Ireland, but this traffic was easier to handle than Dungiven's war job, that of ammunition depot. The small engines permitted were scarcely suited to the transport of bren-guns and the like. Dungiven's only other excitement occurred on the second Tuesday of each month, the occasion of the cattle fair. A light engine would arrive at Limavady from the junction, having piloted the 9.55am ex Derry. Empty wagons were then worked to Dungiven, the special for Derry leaving at 2pm.

DERRY CENTRAL

Although Limavady and its branch to Dungiven had a setting of some scenic beauty and considerable railway interest the operations thereon never seemed, in the enginemen's eyes at any rate, to be pervaded by quite the mystical charm of the Derry Central. One reason for this, I think, was the possibility for men and engines from four different sheds to meet at Magherafelt, a town of some character in South Derry, which in fact took the eventual closures with disappointing composure.

Although the mileposts and bridges were reckoned from the Magherafelt end, I always think of the Derry Central as commencing at Macfin, which was, of course, its junction with the main line. Just south of the station here, a minor road intersects the main line at a level crossing, with the large and genial Mrs Kennedy Clinton in efficient charge. Coming in from the south west, the Derry Central had to cross this road also but, instead of a level crossing, a massive stone bridge was built which remains today, where no track survives.

From Macfin the DC line fell at 1/72 (easing to 1/75) to

the bridge over the Bann, controlled by the Macfin–Garvagh tablet. The line then climbed at 1/131 to Curragh Bridge Halt, a galvanised hut on a platform on the up side. A mile farther on a bank of 8 miles began, not the steepest on the DC but the most persistent. As far as Aghadowey (milepost 68) the upward trend was mostly easier than 1/100. Here an attractive red-brick building on the down side was opposite a siding, worked by the tablet. The line then passed under the road and after a mile steepened to 1/94 until approaching Moneycarrie Halt (66¼), merely a platform on the up side with a wooden hut.

Now the climb was mainly at 1/133 until the line dropped slightly to cross the river Agivey before entering Garvagh (milepost 64). This pleasant station, with red-brick buildings on the down side but merely a waiting hut on the up platform, was about a mile east of the town, from which a journey to Coleraine was 3 miles shorter by road. The signal cabin and goods shed were a short distance to the south, the tablet being issued from the booking office, as at Bellarena on the main line and Dunloy after that cabin was burnt down. Milepost 61½ was the next summit, reached on a 1/118 bank, after which the line fell steeply at 1/75 for 1½ miles and then more easily into Kilrea (58½ miles). By this detour the DC was almost back to the Bann river again, it making some sense in the 1880s for Garvagh, Kilrea and Maghera to be on the one railway line. Kilrea's goods shed and cattle dock were on the town or up side of the line, with a water tank on each platform.

The line now climbed modestly on an embankment to Tamlaght Halt (55¾). Just beyond an accommodation crossing a small platform on the down side had a stone hut on which was inscribed 1911. Inexperienced drivers found this halt very difficult to spot at night, especially if Mary Donnelly had run out of oil and failed to light the lamp. She lived in the adjacent cottage and rarely failed to emerge from it to wave to the crew. Apart from the absence of rails the scene is much the same today, the signpost on the road a short distance

away indicating 'Tamlaght O'Crilly' alongside another evoca-
tive name, 'Killygullib Orange Hall'.

After Tamlaght there was nearly a mile steeply down at
1/90 and then a steady rise through Upperlands (52½) at
1/102. At the Maghera end of this station was a stone bridge
and at the other a goods shed on the down side and a private
siding, worked by the tablet. This line, which then crossed
the village street on its way to Clark's linen mills, was probably the main reason for the survival of the Magherafelt–Kilrea
stub until 1959. In the mill itself shunting was reputed to be
performed by a horse. Stationmaster McWilliams had his
house adjacent to the station buildings and operated the local
post office from there, being thus also postmaster of
Upperlands.

At milepost 50 was the highest town on the line, Maghera,
with staggered platforms, the down one having the station
buildings, today used as council offices. The goods shed and
cattle dock were on the up side and Herbie Wilson was the
stationmaster. The first mile out of Maghera was down a 1/73
gradient and apart from a couple of minor humps it was all
downhill for 5 miles. On one occasion in the early fifties 79,
with a young crew, had been turned at Magherafelt in course
of working empty cattle wagons, so that the return trip would
be uninterrupted. The engine was in poor shape and without
any sanding came to a stand on the bank, less than 2 miles
from Maghera. Soon the crew were receiving advice from
neighbouring farms adjoining the track that the only way to
get moving was to set back for another run at it, which was
indeed how *Kenbaan Castle* got to Maghera that day.

In the up direction tickets were examined at the next
station, Knockloughrim (46¾ miles). Here the line curved
under a stone bridge past a platform on the up side with
buildings in red brick. A Pinkerton box operated a small
siding on this side and the porter in charge, Beatty (nicknamed 'the Admiral') had a home-made tablet for speedy
operation of the points, a most irregular arrangement which,
however, saved time and energy for all concerned.

An iron bridge over the Moyola river soon preceded Bowman's crossing, usually gay with flowers. To driver Jock Duff of Belfast, however, the most colourful aspect of this scene was an orange cat, but his plan to secure a kitten of this ilk was never realised. With poor health, he was also considered a fine engineman, but in my view his dull running provided plenty of scope for feline study en route. Before Magherafelt there was a sharp rise at 1/96 before the line ran down under several bridges in a cutting to join the Cookstown line and terminate at a turntable just beyond the bay platform (page 17)

Derry Central passenger services had best be examined together with those of the Cookstown line, of which it was considered to be a branch. The DC was dominated, nevertheless, by Coleraine and it was mainly from the north it could expect its traffic. All its stations were in County Londonderry, so Derry and Coleraine were the natural business links. Portrush, too, was important, and excursion traffic, including fireworks specials, certainly added to the takings of DC stations. Kilrea expected its goods and perishable traffic from Belfast, not by the shorter Magherafelt route (56 miles) but via Coleraine. For this the 3.30am perishable ex Belfast was the important train, before the war. Later it was the 1.15am goods from which bread came off at Coleraine for the DC. Smaller stations got mails and bread (some from Derry) by way of the 6.45am passenger ex Coleraine. The rest went with the 7.15am goods (5.45 am, postwar).

In 1939 this goods was making a reasonably smart run to Magherafelt in 3hrs 10mins but ten years later it was a much more protracted affair, reaching Magherafelt just before noon after a six-hour journey during which the crews changed at least once. Over the years crews on the passenger workings also exchanged footplates at Kilrea and Maghera and it was typical gamesmanship when approaching, having spotted the other engine already in the station and blowing off strongly, to liven up the fire to have a good head of steam just as the train stopped. Each fireman, from experience, would indeed be optimistic if he expected to find more than a minimum of water in the boiler despite this fine show of steam.

Before the war the job of catering for special traffic from the various fairs was quite considerable, compared with what it had dwindled to by 1950. Kilrea's, on the second and fourth Wednesday of every month, was probably the most important, and shortly after 3pm on such days it was possible to see three engines in Kilrea at the one time. One would have the 2.5pm passenger ex Portrush and another, the 12.30pm goods ex Magherafelt, which on such occasions attached a few six-wheeled carriages at Kilrea so that between there and Coleraine it could run as a mixed train, serving Garvagh and Aghadowey. On these fair days such carriages arrived at Kilrea on a 9.10am special passenger train from Coleraine, calling at all stations. The engine of this then awaited the pleasure of stationmaster Sam Gillen (no relation of the engine driver of the same name at Ballymena). Usually a special of cattle wagons was sent to Magherafelt to connect with the 6pm goods, the engine then returning light to Coleraine, but occasionally a busy fair might warrant a through special to Belfast, with overtime for the crew if the wagons were required the next day and they had to wait till they were washed. On the other hand a very slack fair might result in a few wagons only, which could be attached to the rear of the 2.5pm passenger ex Portrush or the 11.18am ex Magherafelt or even added to the 12.30pm goods. If 56 was on the 11.18am a banker would in these circumstances seem justified but some of the old drivers would be looking for assistance even when they had one of the larger 4-4-0s.

The DC towns were scarcely affected at all by wartime industry but the line was in frequent use by troop trains going to the GNR from the north west, for the GNR Derry line was partly in neutral territory. However, like most parts of Northern Ireland the towns on the line had their allotment of troops, as evidenced by a 10.30pm on Saturdays from Coleraine to Kilrea for servicemen after an evening out. Other extra passenger traffic on this section of line was occasioned by the building of Mullaghmore aerodrome near Aghadowey which required workmen's trains from Coleraine.

Most regular trains on the DC were handled by Coleraine enginemen, through Cookstown and Ballymena crews often worked part of the way to a crossing point. Even the top link at Coleraine usually had one turn up the DC to keep them in touch, but most of the trains were in charge of the Derry Central link, a collection of rare individuals, whom the firemen and cleaners regarded with very mixed feelings. One of these was 'Bulgy' Bill Stewart, corpulent, with a waxed moustache which he flicked quickly with his hand as he spoke. His most regular contribution towards conversation was a high-pitched 'Oh Christ!', but not so very surprising on one occasion when a thunderous blow on the cab-side awakened him suddenly as he dozed on the shunting engine. That inveterate student of human nature, driver Billy McDonald, had sent along his fireman with a hammer, guessing that Stewart was almost certainly asleep, with his head resting on the regulator. Davie Brangam was Stewart's fireman during the early part of the war when Hugh Davidson was head cleaner at Coleraine. One Christmas Eve, after they had brought in their engine, it was soon evident that they had been celebrating more than somewhat along the line. The ever watchful cleaners saw Stewart hide something in the sandbin so they told Davidson. He soon found a large bottle of whiskey and put it away in the press. Then a pot of tea was brewed, but Brangam and his driver, though accepting the invitation to participate, made no mention of the whiskey. When they decided to go home and began to search through the sand, Davidson and the lads greatly enjoyed Stewart's polite and puzzled comments, punctuated by querulous interjections from Brangam, very disappointed indeed with his driver. A fortnight later, coming off the late turn again, they were again invited for tea. Halfway through the refreshment, the head cleaner opened the press, remarking. 'I think you men could do with something a bit stronger.' Thus were Stewart and Brangam permitted to drink their own whiskey.

One of the stories about the DC I like best concerns not a driver but a Coleraine guard, J.B. Parkhill, whose father was signalman at Macfin and whose brother Vic still makes a handsome figure in guard's uniform at Coleraine. Jim was an inveterate fox-hunter at a time when 10s was paid at the police station for every fox's tongue. So, when on the early turn, he would invariably have been out shooting the previous evening, and on his way to the railway next morning would call at Coleraine barracks for payment, with the fox slung over the bar of his bicycle. Once the tongue had been removed he would place the fox's body in the van of the 6.50am to Magherafelt, easing it into the Bann after Macfin. One morning, however, he was preoccupied and did not remember about the fox till he was past Aghadowey, so he had to push the body out onto the permanent way. Shortly afterwards along came the track-walker, who spotted the fox, saw it as a gift from heaven, and trudged with it all the way to Garvagh. He had then another mile to go along Station Road to the police barracks, where a tongueless fox was revealed, with the advice that he could now dispose of the body.

Table F provides reasonable detail of the standard of performance of DC operation. Although *94* had been a daily performer in 1939 on the 6.45am ex Coleraine, postwar appearances by the moguls were rare. Thus to experience the run with *90* was all the more valuable, illustrating a Portrush 'express' using the alternative route. One of the pre-war top link men, Jimmy Gregg, kept very close to booked time throughout, reaching Cookstown Junction only a few seconds after he was booked to pass, and arriving in Belfast dead on time.

A brief look at the engines observed around Coleraine at the time of *90*'s run illustrates that the pre-war situation had, as yet, little altered. 4-4-0 *50* worked the afternoon train from Portrush to Magherafelt and another interesting engine (though not NCC pre-war) was the 0-6-0 tank, *18*, shunting in Coleraine yard. The previous week *15* had been shunting there and *13* had worked a local train from Portrush, *69* going out the DC with the 1.35pm ex Portrush. Later that day *2 Glendun* worked a special from Portrush to Kilrea and another excursion with, presumably, DC interest was for Portadown, worked by *98*.

COOKSTOWN

Cookstown was 54½ miles from Belfast by GNR and after the loopline had been built the NCC distance became 51¼ miles. An early morning goods ran on each route, both engines then working passenger trains out of Cookstown, though the NCC shed housed at least one engine, even as late as 1950. From 1947 the 1.50am Belfast–Cookstown goods (NCC) was rostered for a 2-6-4 tank. Leaving again with the 8am passenger this was the only time of the day a tank engine could be seen between Magherafelt and Cookstown. It seems quite possible that an NCC tank engine had never previously been seen at Cookstown though the GN 4-4-2 tanks reached there quite regularly. Although their trains were slower, the GNR provided slightly better facilities to Belfast, as well as, of course, to Dublin, Derry and the west, but in such matters Great Northern management did tend to be more realistic.

Ten years later the basic passenger service from Belfast to Cookstown and the Derry Central was almost the same as pre-war. The 6.25am ex York Road (5.55am, postwar) to Coleraine had a bogie van and four brown vans (one each for Magherafelt, Cookstown, Draperstown and DC stations) attached to the rear. At Cookstown Junction these were detached and the Ballymena 4-4-0s backed down with two old bogies (a compo and a third) into which passengers had to change. This set went through to Portrush via the Derry Central, passengers for Cookstown having to change again into the 8.11am ex Magherafelt, which had worked out of Cookstown at 7.30am to make a connection into the 6.45am Coleraine–Belfast, via the Derry Central. For its 2½ hour trip the latter had nothing more luxurious than a couple of old bogies attached to a six-wheeled guard's van. The 7.30am set

provided further connecting trains out of Cookstown at
10.20am and 3.45pm and composed of three old bogies (a
compo, a third and a brake third) finished the day at Coleraine after a trip to Portrush on the 5.35pm ex Magherafelt.

The only other passenger working out of Cookstown was
at 12.40pm, the same engine, crew and carriage set returning
from Belfast at 4.20pm. In their turn Sam Stewart, Murray
and Harkness, with their firemen, Cole, Colgan and Nelson,
thus brought a vintage air daily into the rapidly modernising
atmosphere of York Road. By 1938 compounds 56 and 57
were much rarer on this than 'Whippets' such as 24, 65 and
especially 62 but the carriage set seemed never to change
(centre corridor 86, a side corridor compo and an old guard's
van). The 12.40pm usually had a couple of brown vans of
which one was destined for Larne harbour.

The other departures up the DC were the 2.20pm and
6.50pm ex Portrush. The latter went to Cookstown and
simply balanced the 7.30am set, being identical in composi-
tion. The carriages for the 2.20pm usually had more modern
stock, two corridors (a compo and a third) and a bogie guard's
van. This train also included a brown van out of Portrush, collected another at Upperlands and a third (from Cookstown) at
Magherafelt. This set had been the rear portion of the 9.55am
ex Belfast as far as Cookstown Junction. Locomotive variety
was assured, for a Castle normally worked the afternoon train
ex Portrush, whereas the early morning departure up the DC
had a mogul, and the evening one a compound or a 'Whippet'.

The only other passenger workings to be mentioned, pre-
war, were the regular excursions, usually on Fridays and
Saturdays, for shopping in Belfast. The morning one left
Coleraine at 7.55am, empty carriages, and picked up passengers at stations, Aghadowey to Randalstown inclusive. The
afternoon one (Belfast shops remained open till 9pm in those
days on Saturdays) left Coleraine at 2.3pm, reaching Belfast
at 4.31pm. Return times were usually around 6.45pm and
9.15pm, so different crews worked the return trip. Belfast
crews normally travelled down passenger in the morning to

work up the specials with a Coleraine engine, which worked the return services manned by Coleraine men. The trend of the engines used on such excursions can be gathered from the following, from the summer of 1938.

			Driver	
20 August	9.55pm	Belfast–Coleraine via main line	74	W. Piggot
27 August	9.15pm	DC	83	W. Piggot
3 September	9.55pm	main line	83	W. Piggot
10 September	9.15pm	DC	83	J. McClements
	9.55pm	to Ballymena	82	R. McIlhagga
17 September	9.55pm	Belfast–Coleraine via main line	76	J. McClements
23 September	7.20pm	main line	81	J. Barr
24 September	9.15pm	DC	94	D. Ferguson
	9.55pm	to Ballymena	3	D. Boden

Leaving Cookstown Junction (25 miles from Belfast via Greenisland) the Cookstown line climbed modestly for a mile to Doyle's bridge and then ran down, mostly at 1/135, to Randalstown (27 miles). The station buildings and platform were on the up side of the line, as were also a cattle dock and goods shed. Randalstown was the terminus of the line, on the eastern bank of the Maine river, from 1848 till 1856. Although the major part of the town was on the other side, the position of the station was never changed, so it remained just another badly sited station, the signal cabin being closed, so that the tablet section became Cookstown Junction-Toome, 11¼ miles. During World War II a very important petrol depot was nearby in the grounds of Shanes Castle (where today a charming narrow-gauge railway is a new tourist attraction) and the turnover of wagons became so great that the cabin had to be reopened.

The line then crossed over the Maine on a magnificent stone viaduct, to my mind the most aesthetically satisfying on the NCC. Through the Deerpark there was a climb at 1/135 to milepost 29, the highest point of the line before Magherafelt. From this summit the line dropped, with slight undulations, for 8 miles, within sight of Lough Neagh, a tourist area which seemed to make little appeal to NCC management.

The steepest part of the line east of the Moyola river was the 1/132 down through Staffordstown. The siding here was operated by a Pinkerton box, and on the platform could usually be seen the bath which the porter in charge, Charlie Doherty, brother of Paddy, driver at Coleraine, hoped generous enginemen might fill with coal. Before and again just beyond Toome station the track crossed the main road by level crossings. The platform was on the up side and convenient to a hostelry well known to the crews of goods trains. From a goods shed on the down side, tracks led to sidings at the wharf for sand and clay traffic, after which was the Bann bridge and County Derry. Level track through several crossings was followed by the Moyola river, crossed on a fine stone viaduct. From here there was a sharp rise past Nestlé's factory and siding, at 1/89, before the level crossing at Castledawson station, where the grade had now eased to 1/237. Of the two platforms here it was the up one which had the station buildings, with goods shed and yard behind it.

From Castledawson (40½) there was a two mile climb, mainly at 1/101, under bridge 298 to the Chapel Hill, after which the line dropped modestly and over a level crossing into Magherafelt (42¾), below and to the north of that town. Here the booking office, with station buildings, was on the down platform, which was shorter than the island one, the far side of which was called the Derry Central platform, from which trains could not proceed to Cookstown, just as trains for the Derry Central could not depart from the down platform, but had to arrive at the island one. The signal cabin was at the west end of the latter, water tanks being at the same end of the down platform and also in the yard beside the derelict engine shed. On the town side of the station were several sidings and two goods sheds with cattle dock and also the residence of Hugh Moore, the permanent way inspector for No 5 district (the area west of Cookstown Junction and Macfin). Two carriages were standing opposite this house one

day in the late forties when they were run into with such
vigour by 75, just fresh from shops, that one of her buffers
was sent flying into the ditch. The driver involved was the
redoubtable Billy Bankhead of Ballymena. When asked to
attend an inquiry concerning the mishap, he simply announced
that he was guilty. It shows the calibre of the NCC, however,
that this was not just accepted, but in fact investigated until
the blame was laid firmly on the signalman who, after setting
the points differently than for the routine shunt, merely
shouted something at the fireman, instead of making sure
that the driver understood the alteration. From experience
he should have known that co-operation was not over-evident
on this particular footplate.

Leaving Magherafelt the DC and Cookstown lines ran
parallel for a short distance, so that at 8.10am, for instance,
when only a minute separated the two departures, there was
a chance for the crews to enjoy a short race, as was also possible on other Irish railways at Palace East, Clones and
Lavistown Junction.

Before Draperstown Junction there was a slight hump
after which the line fell at 1/185 before a rise at 1/161 to the
summit at 194ft. Nearby, Carmean lime siding, constructed
in 1943, was on the down side and usually shunted by any
available engine at Magherafelt. At Lismoney. before Moneymore, a war department store depot, opened in 1942, brought
considerable activity to the Cookstown line for the remainder
of the war. A Pinkerton box provided entry to a three-line
reception yard with various other offshoots. Here an engine,
invariably a V class 0-6-0, could be 'locked in' much of the
day, shunting, before proceeding with her goods train towards
Antrim, where footplates were exchanged with a down train.

Moneymore (49½ miles) where tickets were examined, had
its single platform and buildings on the down side, with goods
shed and cattle dock opposite, for its active traffic in
livestock. The line then undulated to milepost 52½, from
which it climbed steeply for a mile at 1/99 before falling
under a stone bridge into Cookstown (53¾). After the turn-

table, on the up side, came the single-road engine shed, cattle dock and large goods shed. Between these and the single-platform line was a runround which extended past the end of the station buildings and across Union Street into the market yard, this traffic being usually worked by a horse. During World War II the platform line was also extended to take trains of ten carriages to and from the Great Northern. There was also a short spur on the other side of the platform, used for wagon exchange between the two railways. The 2-4-0 56 had a habit of getting off the road when it ventured into this no-man's land. The adjoining GNR station was slightly farther from the town's main street and had its own turntable, though its engine shed had been long out of use. Possibly the busiest train out of Cookstown was the GNR one on a Sunday night and it was logical that the NCC passenger service should expire 5½ years before its rival. After the war the NCC did not run Sunday trains and even during the thirties it restricted services to a Sunday train to Portrush in the summer, with a connection to Derry.

In 1936 the daily goods left Cookstown at 10.20am, with carriages attached for Magherafelt. Wartime traffic so transformed goods services on the branch that even as late as 1948 there was a 10.30am to Antrim and a 3pm through to Belfast. Even after Kilrea–Macfin closed in 1950 Cookstown still had goods trains out at 10.15am and 1.45pm but by the time Cookstown–Magherafelt closed completely in 1955 there was only one departure, at 10am.

Moneymore had a good fair on the 21st of each month. For this an engine piloted the 6.25am to Cookstown Junction and then the branch train forward to Magherafelt. After the necessary balancing runs with empties, or engine and van, three extra departures from Moneymore emerged on such days. The Cookstown engine left Moneymore at 2pm with stock for that direction, and the fair engine would make a trip to Magherafelt at 1.5pm to connect with the Coleraine goods, held till 1.30pm on such occasions. Finally a through special for Belfast left Moneymore at 2.10pm

The Cookstown line seems to have been fairly free from fatalities. *13* was responsible for one, when descending the bank towards Castledawson with a heavy goods train. Although a boy on the line was observed in good time he ignored frantic whistling and was killed. An unusual engine for this section was *102*, working a wartime special from Portstewart. An American soldier fell to his death at Toome after attempting to open the door, which struck the tablet catcher, driver John McAllister being in no way to blame. With a speed restriction of 45mph, which also applied to the Derry Central, it seemed a pointless decision to erect tablet catchers at Toome, Castledawson, Magherafelt and Moneymore.

Additional services of a non-military nature were also of great interest during the war and it is unfortunate, for instance, that records of the locomotive workings of the Saturdays-only Omagh-Portrush (via Cookstown) train have not survived. A typical Saturday night train of the war period was the 11.32pm from Cookstown Junction to Cookstown, worked by a Ballymena engine and crew and frequently booked to return with the carriages during the small hours. On one occasion three girls, who had been depending on the empty carriage working, found themselves stranded. Bankhead was the driver and he was 'on the carpet' for taking them on the footplate. His explanation was, as usual, fairly unanswerable, 'If they had been your daughters, would you have expected me to leave them behind?'

I once asked an old Cookstown driver what he remembered best about the railway there and his reply was both moving and surprising. 'Coming home with the goods at night we had a siding to shunt near Moneymore. The train could be 60 wagons, so to save the guard a walk I'd put the tablet into the Pinkerton and work the points. Doing this on several occasions of an autumn evening I'd catch the scent of perfume and hear the murmurs of a courting couple. I'd shout to him if he wanted a hand and they'd laugh back but I never actually saw them at any time.'

DRAPERSTOWN

At milepost 44 the Cookstown line passed under a stone bridge, just beyond which was the Pinkerton box for the Draperstown branch. Once the road had been made the train pulled onto the branch and the guard would then phone Magherafelt to this effect. The red-brick house at the junction between the two lines was the home of Andy Carleton, who had once been employed as fireman at Draperstown and in later days, as the crew of the daily goods awaited the guard, Andy would inevitably climb up on the footplate, turn his back on the firebox and comment on the quality of the coal.

Swinging round north west, with Slieve Gallion splendid in the background, the line soon reached a level crossing, through which the downward trend increased to 1/101. After milepost 45, however, a climb commenced which raised the line 166ft in 3½ miles. A mile farther, at Desertmartin, the up grade was 1/113, the last mile to the summit, at 321ft, being at 1/61. It was on this bank during World War II that an engine stalled with empty carriages intended for a major military operation. Desertmartin platform and buildings were on the up side of the line, the man-in-charge being John Crawley, father of Alfie Crawley, driving from Ballymena today and one-time fireman at Cookstown. During World War II the US army had an important stores depot nearby, thus providing, in the evening of its existence, the heaviest traffic the branch had ever known. Although all points off the branch were worked from the branch staff, red and round, trains from Magherafelt direction were warned to approach these facing points with care.

Similarly at Draperstown the porter-in-charge had to ensure that the points there were set for the platform road before the arrival of the daily goods train at the centrally situated station, 271ft above sea level and 50¾ miles from York Road via Greenisland. Here the platform was on the down side, with cattle dock and loading bank opposite. At the end of the spur from the runround which passed the goods shed a line had gone off to a turntable and engine shed, abandoned since

1930. The daily goods, rarely more than six wagons, was
easily handled, but some skill was required at times to haul a
big train of empty wagons from Magherafelt for the monthly
fair. On such occasions a Castle (restricted to 15mph on the
branch) was usually preferred to the usual 'Whippet', and left
Magherafelt with the empties at 11.45am, after piloting the
9.55am passenger ex Belfast. This occurred on the first Friday
of the month, the loaded special being booked to leave for
Belfast at 2pm. The daily goods usually departed from
Draperstown around 10am, having left Magherafelt about
8.30am. For a long period it was possible to witness the
morning goods from Cookstown and that from Draperstown
passing that junction within a few minutes, undoubtedly a
hallowed hour.

One Saturday towards the end of World War II Coleraine
driver Davie Brangam had 66 for the Draperstown goods. The
previous day the same crew had been careful to clear up all
outstanding shunting to leave sufficient time to permit an
expedition into the town for some 'under the counter' food-
stuffs. The porter, 'Yankie' Frank McWilliams, had already
heard about the bread and water diet which thus justified
departure of driver and fireman up the town. However, they
had scarcely left before McWilliams was after them with a
lament about the freezing conditions of the station buildings
so utterly piteous that the idea of a search for extra food took
on the semblance of gross inexcusable self-indulgence. However, the men went their way with the suggestion that
McWilliams help himself to coal from the engine's tender.

Some time later the two shoppers were refreshing themselves at the nearest pub when Frank arrived in a state of
apparent excitement. It seemed that Magherafelt required the
engine and were questioning so much delay at Draperstown
on a quiet Saturday morning. So Brangam and his mate
returned quickly to the station and 66 moved off tender first
with its small train. When the fireman thought of putting a
few shovelfuls on the fire it was immediately apparent that
McWilliams must have spent the entire time taking away coal

in his wheelbarrow. It was just a matter of luck that *66* could return to Coleraine that day under her own steam. It was a month before Brangam was back in Draperstown, by which time there wasn't a trace of coal for anyone to argue about.

In the old days, being appointed to Draperstown had the glamour of martyrdom, for it was a common punishment for some misdemeanour. That the crime was frequently one of an alcoholic nature goes without saying but I am reasonably sure that the air coming off the Sperrins was no sure guarantee of a more sober existence, where the driver had very little to do all day and was finished his day's work before closing time. It is quite remarkable how many surviving enginemen remember cleaning at Draperstown fifty years ago and how much their reminiscenses concern food and especially drink.

Billy Bell (later foreman at Belfast) was the Draperstown driver during World War I, with Billy White, head cleaner, the same man who retired from Magherafelt in the mid fifties. Bell had a large family, who entertained the various young cleaners temporarily loaned to the shed. Apart from musical evenings many a lad thus sampled his first bottle of stout, and this was always the reward for a thorough job of cleaning an engine which, with a maximum daily mileage of forty-eight, can never have been very dirty. The old 2-4-0s *1* and *2* were both shedded there at one time.

After a time a driver named Frew was involved in a disgraceful episode on the narrow **gauge**, whereby both driver and fireman were so drunk that one fell off the engine. Bell was sent to replace him and for a time Draperstown had Bob McKenzie, later a noted top link driver at Belfast. By this time Bell had decided that far from being a punishment, Draperstown was really an excellent place and applied to get back to it.

BALLYCLARE

Here was a town of 4000 inhabitants, twelve miles by road from Belfast. Neither its broad-gauge line to reach Belfast nor its narrow gauge ever looked like surviving the motor age and, in fact, when the passenger service on the former was abandoned in 1938 after a life of fifty-four years there were only three trains daily, the quickest taking 31min from Belfast and 28min from Ballyclare. This was fast compared to the situation before the building of the loopline when Greenisland had first to be visited.

So the NCC buses could make the run as quickly as the trains and the management saw no need to give Ballyclare a good commuter service later by fast train when they had the traffic anyway. Even the goods service ceased a few months after the passenger but was revived with a vengeance during the war, after which a twice-a-week goods train sufficed till 1950, when there was final closure.

The branch deviated from the main line a short distance before Kingsbog Junction cabin, the signalman having a special path cut across the bog to deliver the tablet to the crew, already some 50 yards onto the branch. After a level crossing the line rose sharply for a short distance at 1/102 to the summit, 358ft above sea level and the highest point of the entire NCC broad gauge. There was then a fall at 1/147 under the Doagh-Greenisland road to Lisnalinchy Halt (13¼ miles). Towards Ballyclare this steepened to 1/77, easing considerably near the terminus.

At the end anything smaller than the mogul type was permitted on the branch, but the 2-4-0 tanks appear to have predominated on the passenger turns till 1930. Later, any of the smaller classes, often 2-4-0s, or a Castle running out its mileage might appear on the branch. The 5.30am goods ex Belfast provided the engine for the 7.5am passenger ex Ballyclare which had slight pretension to being a fast train in that it did not call at Lisnalinchy Halt (near a race track) and ran in from Monkstown in 11 min. When one considers the tonnage of the BCDR surburban trains of the same period the size of this 7.5am shows how completely hope had been abandoned, for accommodation was one bogie only, old *24*, which could, if necessary, be replaced by identical *31*. Both

had all three classes of accommodation *and* two lavatories in
a mere 22 ton vehicle. This, together with a four-wheel van
made up the entire train and also the 1.25pm ex Ballyclare,
the balancing workings being at 10.5am and 6.20pm from
Belfast, the engine of the latter hauling the 7pm goods to
Ballyclare Junction, whence it ran light to Greenisland. The
only other train, the 3.20pm ex Belfast (1.40 on Saturdays)
had just one vehicle, a tri-compo brake of corridor type which
returned as the 5.35pm to Belfast.

From early in the war Ballyclare became a large depot for
the Royal Engineers and goods traffic became extremely
heavy. To safeguard such trains on the steep approach to
Ballyclare the usual fixed distant signal was replaced by
a warning board enforcing a full stop before the first siding
was reached. Trains leaving Ballyclare were often in some
trouble. On one occasion a train of bren-guns for Portrush
could not surmount the 1/77 even though *2 Glendun* with
driver Fillis had the assistance of *71* driven by John Redfern
of Belfast. Even after another engine had arrived from Belfast
the trio could not get the train up to Lisnalinchy. Eventually
94, working up on a mainline goods with Johnny McAuley,
was halted at Kingsbog, and though the mogul should not
have entered the branch it was only through her aid that the
train was got on the move.

Ballyclare layout was very simple, with a platform and
building on the down side, with engine runround. Opposite
was a goods shed with several long sidings. Some of the
building and the platform form the bus station of this
pleasant town today and the gentlemen's lavatory, apparently
unaltered from the thirties, is still in daily use.

CHAPTER 3

Locomotive Heritage

Although this book has as its main theme the NCC locomotive story during its last twenty-three years (the period of the Ulster Transport Authority and its successor, Northern Ireland Railways), for better understanding it has been necessary to refer back in some detail. Some might say, indeed, that the period since 1948, despite its great interest, has been merely a running down process of greater days.

The observant traveller of the period around World War I would probably have come away from the NCC with two main conclusions about its locomotives: that this was a most unorthodox and individual railway, and that it seemed to avoid the obsession that a leading bogie is essential for passenger work. That other Midland, based on Broadstone in Dublin, was probably the nearest in its liking for the 2-4-0 type and it is of interest to note that some years later both took a 2-6-0 as their standard type for their most important trains. In 1920 the NCC had twenty-five 2-4-0s as against twenty-two 4-4-0s. Their engine total (broad gauge) has usually been between sixty-five and seventy, and at that point in time sixteen 0-6-0s almost completed the picture, apart from a few 2-4-0 tanks.

The incidence of the huge LMS overlordship did not materially affect the situation for they undoubtedly had their own problems. With an apparent conviction that the 4-4-0 type was large enough for most LMS requirements it was hardly to be expected that anything larger would be authorised for the NCC. So an improved version of the U class, the U2, became a basis for a standardisation process which seemed to have been timed for completion just in time for another war. Nevertheless, even in 1938 there were still a few relics of NCC eccentricity, so in starting with them and ending with the moguls the full position that year is now described.

Both railwayman and enthusiast alike seem to have been fascinated by the two 4-4-0s with 7ft drivers, *50* and *55*. The NCC thought of them as the fastest engines in Ireland, but this seems extremely unlikely and there are certainly no statistics of performance to justify such a claim. Both had commenced in 1895 as 2-4-0s, but had shown a tendency to hunt at speed. Fitted with bogies two years later they now had a weight of 46 tons 9cwt. Thus it was still as a 2 cylinder compound that *50, Jubilee*, became the first engine in 1924 to use the new bridge over the Bann at Coleraine. Two years later she was converted to a simple engine with 19in x 24in cylinders and superheated 4ft x 4½in boiler, 170lb pressure and shedded at Larne. With Derby chimney and Crewe type framing (page 36) she now seemed indeed to embody the LMS, in which those two famous railways had dominant influence. Now class D1, this engine spent most of 1938 lying at York Road out of steam, but the war soon changed that. In October 1939 she emerged from the 'shops in black livery with a reconditioned boiler off V class 0-6-0 *13* and ran over 200,000 miles more to finish in October 1946 with 1,561,442 miles. On 12 September 1944 I noted her on the 5.30pm local Belfast-Carrickfergus but she could turn up almost anywhere, even the Limavady branch and especially, towards the end, the Aldergrove-Ballymena train.

In contrast *55*, when she finished her life in September 1944 with 1,301,142 miles, was still a 2 cylinder compound, 18in and 26in x 24in. *Parkmount* still carried a 4ft 4in boiler, 170lb pressure. Shedded at Cookstown in the early thirties, this engine was quite active in 1938, being apparently the first choice if one of the Larne railcars had to be replaced, but since 1935 when her tender was fitted with a weatherboard, she was also familiar on the Limavady branch. An ideal job for her was the 8am ex York Road, which duty she performed on 20 September 1938, with Jimmy Gourley driving. This train called everywhere to Killagan (strange choice) where the engine ran round, working back into Ballymena as a feeder for the 8.15am ex Derry. *55* scarcely moved the following year and not at all during 1940, so apparently the accountant made a strong complaint about engines which exist on paper only. In mid-1942 Malcolm Patrick put *55* through the 'shops and the story goes that he brought this accountant along to have a look at a 'paper' engine.

Another small but famous passenger class were the charming F class 2-4-0s. Not even the war could justify their retention much longer though all three had worked in 1938 and *23* was not finally withdrawn till November 1942. *45* and *46* first appeared in 1880, their inside frames contrasting with the numerous G class 2-4-0s of a few years previously. The F class had at first 16in x 22in cylinders, increased on first rebuild to 17in x 24in. The other engine, *23*, was built in 1885, all three engines remaining simple all their lives, with 6ft driving wheels. These locomotives were only 37½ tons weight, with a 4ft 1in boiler and a tiny tender of only 1456 gallons' capacity

However, *46* received the so-called 5ft boiler in 1928, which certainly did not improve her appearance. Now class F1, this engine put up 12,130 miles during 1938, almost entirely in the process of shunting Belfast passenger yard (usually calculated at 5mph). She was withdrawn that September, three months after *45*, whose tender then went to *23*. This survivor was also mainly used for shunting during 1938 and was withdrawn at the end of 1940. However, she had to be resurrected in July 1941, when the engine position was at its worst, and survived another sixteen months. *23*'s final mileage was 1,580,296, less than either of her sisters, of

which *45* was slightly the more travelled with 1,672,845 miles.
None of these three engines was ever named but *45* carried
for many years a replica of the Prince of Wales's feathers
up on her cab side, having worked the royal train in her first
year. At that period these three were the crack BNCR engines,
working through to Derry daily.

Differing from the F class in cylinders and motion only
were the class C or 'Light' compounds, a seven strong fleet of
2-4-0s, of which only three had survived as such into 1938.
Almost alone then did *56* provide the vintage BNCR atmosphere. Even a visit to the 'shops in September 1937 had left
her virtually just as built. This involved a 4ft 1in boiler, 160lb
pressure, 16in and 23¼in x 24in cylinders and, of course, 6ft
drivers for a total weight of 37 tons 6cwt. During 1938 this
engine was shedded at Cookstown and the following year got
the tender off *46*. Her last days were as Coleraine's shunting
engine. She would then still make an occasional trip to
Portrush on a local train but her most arduous tasks around
that period were her visits to Coleraine harbour. The outward
passage was easy enough and *56* was quite able for the maximum load (propelled) of twenty wagons to the harbour. Much
of the traffic at that time was ammunition, which had to be
hauled up to Coleraine goods yard for making up into a big
train to be worked to some secret destination. *56* was able to
manage six loaded wagons up to the main station if she got a
clear road over the level crossing but if she had to shut off
before this she was in considerable trouble. This little branch
had a round brass staff instead of a tablet and if Tom
Dinsmore, the signalman, stopped them too often, the crew
might retaliate by heating up the staff in the firebox so that
when he grabbed it he burnt his hands. When finally withdrawn in November 1942 *56* had run 1,203,589 miles.

The other two surviving 2-4-0s were now classified C1 since
fitted with the '5ft' boiler, also used to rebuild some engines
of classes B,F,G, and K. In actual fact the diameter of this
boiler was 4ft 8¼in (inside, first ring). *57* was the first engine
in the world to be fitted with a 'Ross' type safety valve (the

inventor lived in Coleraine). Most engines received names during the 1929-32 period though that bestowed on *57* after rebuilding in 1931 was second hand, having previously been borne by the first BNCR compound, *33*. Prior to 1929 the NCC had only five named locomotives and it has always been confusing (if indeed much about the NCC was simple) to have a standard class of 4-4-0s named after castles and also one 2-4-0. However she was the one 2-4-0 to receive the LMS type chimney, as borne by the new 4-4-0s, thus making her easily discernible from *51* (page 17).

During the summer of 1936 there was a Sunday turn to Portrush from Cookstown often worked by *57*. This 9.15am was rostered for one of the standard sets of three old bogies, about 67 tons tare, but if the day promised to be fine carriages off Cookstown's other (Belfast) set might be added. More important in the minds of the crew, however, was the fact that *57* had later to work the 1.10pm Portrush-Derry because on a Sunday at that time of day the only other engines in steam in the Portrush area were moguls, unsuited to Derry's turntable. So *57* worked to Derry and then had to return with the 5.35pm express, as far as Coleraine. This was normally only three bogies, including a tea car, but its tight timings were quite enough for old *57* despite her big boiler with 170lb pressure. It is stimulating today to think of a two-cylinder compound of such antiquity working a main-line express, with refreshment facilities, during the mogul era.

Both *56* and *57* and also, indeed, *58* (later used for the construction of 4-4-0 *28*) were shedded at Larne before World War I, *57* being remembered as the engine in charge of Winston Churchill's train when he was pelted with tomatoes at Larne Harbour in 1912. Undoubtedly these engines were admirable for stopping trains with light loads, the slow beat giving quite an erroneous impression of modest acceleration. There is an entertaining recollection by the late driver Keenan (of Cookstown Junction) of taking seventeen wagons to Draperstown with *56* during the mid thirties. By the time he reached Magherafelt he was looking for water.

However, as he puts it himself, both the columns there were surrounded by brown vans so he completed the journey of nearly 50 miles on less than 1500 gallons. For the return trip he found himself with no less than twenty-nine wagons and van out of Magherafelt. Harkness was there with a 'Whippet' but ever since the strike few railwaymen wanted any truck with Cookstown drivers. Indeed, on one inflamed occasion the 'strike committee' had arrived at Cookstown and one of their number, finding his own brother about to take out an engine, had been prevented from committing murder only by the arrival of the police.

Bearing all this in mind and also the fact that a bad 'Whippet' was worse than any compound, Keenan held on to 56 and despite a stop at Antrim for water, thus preventing a good run at Templepatrick bank, he managed to get the little engine over the summit with this substantial train. Around the same period I observed 57 arrive at Dungannon (GNR) with the 8.50am ex Cookstown and apparently this was a regular working for a period. For the actual performance of both 56 and 57 on passenger workings, the reader should refer to Table F.

The remaining compound in existence in 1938 was 54, class E1 0-6-0. More than twenty years before, this engine and her sister 53 had been stationed in Derry for the through goods to Belfast. The mixed traffic locomotive was much less prevalent in those days and 53, with Joe Kealy firing to John Rafferty, and 54, with Jimmy Logue firing to Jimmy Dennison, worked right through to Belfast, returning next day with the down goods. Like the 2-4-0 compounds already mentioned they had Walschaert's motion and after 53 was scrapped in 1934, 54 became the last two-cylinder goods compound extant in the British Isles by 1937. As rebuilt in 1907 she had the 5ft boiler, with cylinders 18in and 26in x 24in, weighing 43 tons 11cwt. Though smaller than the V class (the 5ft 2½in drivers were the same) 54 was quite an impressive looking engine but sufficiently run down in 1938 to have covered only 6912 miles that year, mainly on work of special type, such as ballasts. She seems to have had something of a comeback the following year by doubling this but did not turn a wheel in 1940, before being withdrawn in September. However, as with *23* and *55*, shortage of motive power caused her to be put back into service again on 1 January and she ran another valuable 65,668 miles before finishing in September 1944 with a total of 1,399,267 miles.

Before turning to the more modern engines it might be as well to mention the various old 0-6-0s surviving in 1938. These were *30, 31, 43* and *44,* survivors of seven class K engines. Every engine already mentioned has been a product of Beyer Peacock and it is only with *43* and *44* that we come to the sole surviving connection of the B&NCR with the firm of Sharp, Stewart & Company. These two engines dated back to 1875-6 and had 17in x 24in cylinders for a 4ft boiler with 5ft 2in drivers. When the new shed at Cookstown Junction went into use in 1911 the two engines shedded there were *44* and *36*, the latter a slightly smaller class of 0-6-0. Parts of a similar engine, *38*, were later combined with *44* and given the latter number, being finally withdrawn with *30* in June 1938, by which time all four engines had the '5ft' boiler.

43 was withdrawn at the end of 1938 with a mileage of 1,604,494 but *31* continued to work till August 1947, mileage 1,764,562. This was the engine on which Tommy McClelland, well known express driver of the thirties, had fired in his youth. Frank McKay, who had been her driver at one period, had been killed in York Road yard by a loose shunted van. During their last years these engines were concerned mostly with shunting and local goods and especially the Carrickfergus harbour line. However, in 1945, with such a shortage of engines, *31* was occasionally pressed into working a passenger local, something one seldom saw her do in the thirties.

So far I have been discussing engines which many of my readers may never have seen. However, in covering the 0-6-0s of 1938 the V class must be mentioned and one of these, rebuilt, did survive till 1964. These were superheated 0-6-0s of 1923, built at Derby, which ran for a few months as *X, Y* and *Z* before being renumbered *13,14* and *15* in April of that

63

year. With boiler, cylinders and motion interchangeable with the two U class 4-4-0s of the previous year they weighed 47 tons 15cwt. 19in x 24in cylinders left them quite a powerful engine and the standard goods driving wheel for the NCC of 5ft 2½in also permitted brisk running.

During their first ten years the V class were very busily employed, both *13* at Cookstown Junction and *15* at Whitehead having duties which involved passenger work and pick-up goods. However, by 1938 many of the engines already described as about to be scrapped were nevertheless more active than the V class, whose fireboxes were now in a bad state, except *14*, which had had some attention in 1935. *13* did not run at all during the years 1935-7 nor did *15* in 1937-8. Eventually these two engines were fitted with reconditioned boilers off *72* and *73*, rebuilt to class U2 in 1937. *14* was very active in 1938, running 32,584 miles and being the invariable engine for the 7.45pm goods from Belfast to Ballymena, driver McAllister or Gray. This had a pilot to Ballyclare Junction (usually the 4-4-0 for the 9.5pm to Larne) and after being overtaken at that outpost by the 8.50pm passenger, followed it on the block to Ballymena. In August 1943 *15* was overhauled at Dundalk after the other two had managed to get attention at York Road works.

Turning now to the passenger engines which had the LMS look, the 'Whippets' must come first in that the engines out of which they were built actually belonged to the turn of the century, the light compounds in fact being pure B&NCR products, before the Midland Railway bought the Irish railway out in July 1903. At once we seem to be in a world of fantasy, of rebuilding, renumbering, reclassifying which, though for the sake of standardisation only, seems merely to complicate the situation.

Class B3 (the Counties) began with *28* in 1927, followed by *21* the following year, both engines having started as class C compounds. The other three B3 engines (*24, 60* and *61*) derived from class B compounds, whose only original difference was that they were always 4-4-0s, not 2-4-0s as had been *21* and *28* (numbered *51* and *58*). By 1938 these five engines had 18in x 24in cylinders and 8in piston valves, retaining, of course, the standard 6ft driving wheels. The last two engines, *60* and *61*, had the considerable advantage of 200lb pressure boilers, the other three having only 160lb.

The other so-called 'Whippets', the class A1 4-4-0s, with lower-pitched boiler, did not give quite the same impression that they were about to take off, but their essential dimensions were the same, all this class having been built out of 'Heavy compound 4-4-0s' of 1902-8. How long the NCC modernisation plan intended either class to last is hard to say, despite the legend on their building plates which in 1938 suggested, for instance, that Binevenagh was only six years old, much as the PP 4-4-0s of the GNR (far better engines) got new building plates at about the same time. However one regards their actual age, the heavy war traffic seemed to reveal their weaknesses more than most. Before the war there had been too many trains of 70-80 tons really to test them. Some of the pathetic performances of the 1940-48 era were just as much due, however, to canny old drivers like Jimmy Gourlay of Ballymena who saw how easy the schedules were and made no attempt to improve on them. 'Half a that 'll dae me,' he would say to his fireman, filling a boiler or shovelling some coal into the firebox.

Table F has most of the logs showing 'Whippet' performance, and a few other snippets of information have been also gleaned from an early log-book compiled by Andrew Donaldson, to give some idea of the running of a few other small engines not shown in the tables. Several of these runs were made on the 11.30am ex Derry during the years 1936-8 when the load was a handy one of two side corridors, a compo-teacar (class G1) and at least one brown van. With 150 tons *34* ran from Castlerock to Coleraine in 8min 49sec, maximum 54mph; *28* managed the same speed when the load was 130 tons for a time of 8min 45sec. It was possibly the better boiler of *61* which enabled her to achieve, for the same section, a time of 7min 51sec, maximum 58mph, with 140 tons. An excursion of seven old bogies, hauled by *21*, made a time of 8min 10sec, maximum 55mph. In the same area but on the Portrush branch, *68*, with only the 160lb boiler, had a nine bogie train from Coleraine to Portrush, so in the circumstances times of 8min 53sec to Portstewart and 7min 23sec forward to Portrush were by no means bad. In the other direction a bright triviality involved three bogies hauled by a 2-4-0, *46*, times being 5min 50sec to Portstewart and a maximum of 55mph for a time into Coleraine of 4min 43sec.

During the thirties Belfast had a few 'Whippets' in addition to a couple at Larne, the daily arrival from Cookstown also having one from time to time, especially during latter days. So one very seldom saw at Belfast those working in the Northern area, which usually included *60, 64* and *66* in addition to the four already mentioned for their performance around Coleraine. The jobs around Belfast were usually rather more onerous and in 1938 three engines with the 200lb boiler were active there, *33* at York Road and *58* and *69* at Larne. *24* and *65* were also mainly used from Belfast in a spare capacity, and *62* was at Cookstown. *28* did not even last into the war period, for she was withdrawn in December 1938, after only 285,421 miles in her final eleven year phase as class B3. Her sister, *21*, lasted somehow till 1947 though in July 1936 this engine had been withdrawn from service. Four months after this she was surprisingly resurrected. The NCC were never in peacetime looking for engines in November so one must assume some kind of game was being played with the accountants. However, during the war it happened again, *21* being withdrawn in September 1940 but put back into stock again the following July.

The modernisation and standardisation of NCC locomotives really begins with the arrival of three G7 boilers from Derby in 1923. Two of these were used to transform two old 'light' compounds (*59* and *62*) into class U1, later to be named after Glens in County Antrim. Henceforward, with one or two minor exceptions all boilers were LMS standard ones (G6, G7 and G8) and could be more economically dealt with at Derby, whence they would be returned in four or five months with new firebox fitted so that the boiler could be put into the next suitable engine coming into the works.

The Glens were regarded, possibly because of their identical boiler, as being of similar power to the class U2 4-4-0s, though they had, of course, an inch less in cylinder. In 1945/6 both *72* and *81* had their cylinders reduced to the 18in x 24in of the Glens and possibly *72*'s were taken off *Glenaan*, just withdrawn. *1* and *2* were not only the first two maroon engines on the NCC but they were the first to have the typical Midland (LMS) look of the twenties. In 1926 and 1931 when the class was completed the parts (page 17) used were also off 'light' compounds but 2-4-0s were used for *3* and *4*.

By 1938 *1-3* were nicely shedded at Ballymena with *4* in Belfast as spare engine. Their duties included shunting in Ballymena goods yard, and local goods work on the Cookstown line. They did have one rather more glamorous duty, however: the Larne harbour coaches from Ballymena off the 4pm ex Derry. Leaving Ballymena at 5.45pm only 54min were allowed for the 44¼ miles, smart work even with a trivial load. This very important train reached its peak during the war, of course, after which it gradually faded in importance until one leaves Derry today at 3pm to arrive in Larne harbour at 6.13pm after a change at Belfast, 193min from Derry. For at least ten years the postwar steam timing was just under 3 hours, via the 'back line', whereas the fastest ever 1939 timing had been 159min.

The kind of operation involved in this fast timing in 1939 is remarkable enough to justify description in detail. Out of Derry it was usually eight vehicles: two corridor thirds, teacar compo, bogie van and two brown vans for Belfast and for Larne harbour brake compo and bogie van. At 4.30pm an even more varied train left Portrush. At the front (for Belfast) was a corridor third and a brake compo and at Coleraine the mogul, which worked through from Portrush to Belfast, placed these on the front of the vehicles from Derry. Next in the train from Portrush was the local set of three old bogies, required for the 5pm local back from Coleraine to Portrush. Finally in the train from Portrush was a brake compo for Larne harbour, placed, at Coleraine, on the rear of the 4pm, which sat only 5min at Coleraine. If one was of an adventurous nature it was possible to stay with the 4pm right through to Belfast, catch the 6.25pm boat express there, and reach Larne Harbour also in time to cross to Stranraer.

To find this working out in practice we can refer to a journey on 2 July 1936, when the load out of Coleraine was eight bogies and two brown vans, a bogie less than the 1939 arrangement. This tonnage is actually on the light side compared to the average 3.15pm load for a dozen or more years after the war and it is interesting to note that *95* lost 1¾min on the hard 25min timing of before the war between Ballymoney and Ballymena. This meant that *Glenaan* (Table L) was starting away with the possibility of a signal check as early as Ballymena Goods, which in fact was cleverly avoided by slow running. *3* ran well after Cookstown Junction, passing Greenisland as booked and reaching Larne Harbour in 51½ minutes.

During 1938 *2* and *3* were the most frequent performers on this turn, the other workings of which were the 7.25pm ex Larne Harbour (another fast train) and finally the 8.50pm Belfast–Ballymena. With the outbreak of war the cosy Ballymena setup gradually changed and the Glens began to work from other sheds, such as Larne and Coleraine. *3* had been the last to receive a name and she was the first to go (October 1946) after a period of shunting and Larne line locals. Her 1926 firebox was finished, but the other three did get a change of boiler, *1* getting *76*'s in 1938 and *2* getting one off *83* in 1941. All four engines ran over **40,000** valuable miles in 1942, *1* finishing with the most (645,922 miles) in April 1947 when withdrawn. Although the tanks were already on order, *4* received a reconditioned boiler off *70* in December 1945 and ran another 3½ years, first from Larne shed and later, renumbered *4A*, between Coleraine and Derry, finishing up at Ballymena in April 1949, with 575,417 miles.

Page 69 *(above)* Castlerock, 19 June 1957. *Chichester Castle* with
5.29pm ex Coleraine (3.40pm ex Belfast); *(below) 79 Kenbaan
Castle* between the two tunnels near Downhill with the 1.15pm
Portrush-Londonderry. 16 August 1938

Page 70   (above) Carrichue, 1956. *The Foyle* passing along the fringe of
Lough Foyle with the 1.5pm Londonderry-Belfast; *(below)*
Waterside, Londonderry, 22 June 1957. *King Edward VIII*
about to depart with the 7.35pm (Saturdays only) to Belfast

In 1938, and indeed for another twelve years, the largest class numerically on the NCC were the U2 4-4-0s, their general nickname, the 'Scotch' engines, being accurate for less than half the class in much the same way as there were less genuine 'Whippets' (class B3) than the rather similar looking A1 class, similarly nicknamed. All eighteen 'Castles', though differing slightly in appearance had, until 1945, the same power output, the only dimensional difference being caused by six boilers, identical, except that the opportunity had been taken for the first time with a Derby boiler (apart from the moguls) to use the wider gauge to full advantage for a wider firebox. The first two of these boilers (classified G7A) were fitted to 'Heavy' compounds *67* and *59* when they were used to construct two more class U2 engines, *85* and *86*. Two years later four more of this type of boiler were ordered (the last new 4-4-0 boilers on the NCC) and when *87* was constructed out of *63* and *72* and *73* rebuilt from class U to U2 they were so fitted. The remaining one was presumably the spare one essential for speedy shopping of engines but was immediately put into *78*.

Chichester Castle was the last of the 1924 Glasgow engines, but when she received this new boiler in October 1936 had run a considerably greater mileage (442,681) than any of her sisters, including the Belfast built *79-81*. Apart from the slight difference in the cab the superb external finish of *74-8* seems to have given them at the time an advantage in prestige over the three Belfast-built engines, though the final allocation to the top-link drivers up to the arrival of the moguls does not show this. Murphy and McCall drove *74*, Campbell and Nixon *78*, McAllister and Kealy *79* and John Young and McKenzie *81*. Some years later when it was decided to name them it was said that Carrickfergus Castle got her name because Young came from that town, where, indeed, his father and brother had driven. Old Stewart Young had for years driven *6*, one of the old outside-framed 2-4-0s, the motion of which he would examine, with lamp between his teeth, while a run was in progress. Another of this class, *29*, the Ballymena shunting engine, had been frequently called into use during the period when the rather erratic 'compounders' monopolised main line expresses, but later with the 'Scotch' engines, failures were very few.

When these top-link drivers at Belfast had to take, reluctantly at first, the moguls, after 1933, *74* and *81* went to Coleraine, where they were still in 1938, almost all the others (except *70, 73* and *80* at Larne) being at Belfast. As more moguls arrived the mileage of the Castles decreased, especially in the winter, but *76*, with drivers McNally and McCrory, and *72*, driven by Patterson and White, were in a regular link at York Road for Larne line workings. *72* and *73* had just been rebuilt, of course, but *73* gave much trouble with hot boxes and so was transferred to Larne, where that fine fitter Jimmy Meneilly soon cured her troubles and she remained at that shed during the whole war period. Another Belfast engine in constant use was *75,* driven by Johnny McAuley and Joe Shiels and used principally on the main line jobs. She was in good repair in 1938, as was *76*, just given a reconditioned boiler off *78*. Of the first five *76* was easily the heaviest in coal, but all were considered better engines than *82-3*, which had gone into service several months before the first Belfast built U2, *79*. In November 1924, after *78* and before *79-83*, *70* had been rebuilt into class U2. It had been 1927 before *71* was also altered to class U2, and 1929 before parts of 'Heavy compound' *20* had been used to produce *84*. Drivers at Belfast in 1938 already mentioned, such as McAuley and McCrory, were, with others such as Mackarell and Rogers, transferred to Coleraine during the exodus of men and engines which followed the Blitz, others to go to a country shed being McNally, Gilmore and Bankhead.

The earliest of all the runs in the log tables occurred in 1932, and therefore prior to the opening of the loop-line and the advent of the moguls. It provides the slightly disappointing information that the Castles, though able for the schedules with fairly light trains, were doing running of a calibre scarcely as good as the 2-6-4 tanks were doing at the very end, when they were falling asunder. On this occasion *34* took over from *75* at Greenisland for the run into Belfast, achieving 65mph in the process. As if to defy traditional NCC procedure this engine, which had been the first 'Heavy compound' and named *Queen Alexandra*, kept the same number during both her time as class A (page 18) and later renewed as Class A1. However, a year after this run she was renamed *Knocklayd*, in keeping with the other 'mountains' of this class.

The fastest timing in 1932 for Portrush expresses was 82 min for the 58.3 miles from Greenisland to Portstewart. Table D shows another Castle successfully keeping a similar timing to the same point, but from York Road, 4¼ miles farther. This was a good solid run but a much more startling affair appeared in a railway magazine of the period, when *79* reached 75mph at Dunadry, maintained 62mph over Cookstown Junction hump, and with an average of 64½mph between Glarryford and Coleraine, which included 76mph down Ballyboyland bank, seemed to justify an estimated net time of 70min. The load seems to have been about six bogies, an undistinguished comment being that the start out of York Road was slower than a mogul because of larger driving wheels. This shows quite a common fallacy whereby the Castles are regarded as an Irish equivalent of the LMS 2P class 4-4-0s, with which they had a really very little in common. This whole run seems to have been a very exceptional effort indeed by the crew, but then Jimmy Marks, with Billy Hanley firing, was quite capable of responding to a special situation. His run in Table G is in singular contrast, one of the very few occasions after 1937 when a 4-4-0 would have been taken for a Portrush train. *71*, just ex-works, with the reconditioned boiler off *84*, performed rather modestly, but the condition of most moguls around that period might not have resulted in anything better.

W.J. Bradley was another well known Belfast driver of the pre-war period, his particular speciality being water colours. These were not always of engines, of course, but one in particular of *70* is remembered rather than his tragic death. This engine was not the most popular of her class, because of her short footplate, left unaltered after rebuilding into class U2. That foot less meant this engine was very warm to ride in the summer, and the position of the reversing lever was so cramped that in certain positions the driver was in danger of a crushed hand.

Although not straying far from Belfast in 1938 *77* spent most of her life at Coleraine, usually as spare engine, so it was apt that she should be working a Coleraine-Magherafelt passenger train on the day the Derry Central closed (page 124). Rather a weak engine, requiring a notch more than most of the other 'Scotch' engines for the same work, she figures in quite a good run in Table N. *82* was another engine regularly used out of Derry but in 1938 was fairly inactive, being due for 'shops, where she got a reconditioned boiler off *1*.

Until *94* became in 1938 the first mogul to be shedded outside Belfast (Coleraine) *81* was the regular engine for the 6.45am Coleraine-Belfast via the DC. The return working was the 9.55am which called at every station from Dunadry to Coleraine except Macfin, and this train included the Royal Mail sorting coach, which was attached for the return journey to the 5.35pm ex Derry. This train was known as 'the Heysham' and served most stations including Macfin, where a connection was taken off the DC. In modern times the 5.30 pm express ex Derry continued to be so called, but a stopping train from Coleraine at 7.7pm had more genuine similarity.

During the busiest years of war haulage the 'Castles' performed noble service, a typical job being the military train from the GNR. Having worked eight bogies from Antrim to the summit, a stop would be made at Ballyclare Junction to attach some carriages from Derry or even Cookstown, detached from a previous train. *81* or *86* were familiar engines on this turn and trains of twelve bogies or even more could be seen arriving at Larne Harbour.

Before leaving the 4-4-0 type a very brief mention should be made of the use of GNR locomotives on excursions to the NCC. A later chapter will refer to both U and S class 4-4-0s of the GNR, but during the thirties it was the Q class which appeared in Portrush quite frequently during the summer on excursions. The 1936 example in Table I shows this class tackling a good sized train in quite admirable style. The restrained speed in the Cullybackey area suggests hand tablet exchange but this was the year when several of this class at Adelaide shed were first fitted with the NCC tablet catcher.

In now coming to the 1938 mogul situation we have a very straightforward story compared to that of the various 4-4-0s. By that summer ten of this class were available, for 99 had gone into service the previous May. Almost a year previously a large tender had arrived from Crewe (very similar to what was now being provided for the 'Black fives') and this was given to 99. The high curved sides were the most obvious change, so that an additional two tons of coal and 1000 gallons of water improved a situation where the first batch of moguls had a tender which held only five tons of coal, the 2500 gallons of water being even slightly less than some of the 4-4-0s. It was said that this large tender was to permit of a double run to Portrush, if necessary. This could be trans-lated as either 260 miles on one tender of coal or 130 miles without taking water (both rather optimistic) but another view was that the alteration was simply to improve appear-ance. But in my opinion, if the moguls had any beauty at all it was with the small tender and the Fowler type chimney. The engine crew was probably not too much concerned either with appearance, or a 'double run'. Probably the driver pre-ferred the older model as it was much more draught-free. His fireman could agree with this except that the new tender made firing less laborious for a tall man, the shovelling plate being level with the firehole and not below it. Another slight altera-tion was that *99-104* had 138 small tubes instead of 121, as in *90-98* but there was a certain amount of interchanging of boilers in latter days, of course, *91* and *93*, for instance, ending up the revised type, with which the tanks too were fitted when they came.

The policy of the authorities, despite having so many good 4-4-0s, was obviously to get the maximum use possible out of the 2-6-0s. The postwar standard of a trip to Portrush and back as a day's work for a mogul crew was not quite good enough for the enterprising Malcolm Speir. Thus one turn in 1938 involved working both the 6.30am to Larne and back and then the 9.45am to Portrush and back. There were ten crews and five moguls in the link responsible for this job but another mogul (not surprisingly *99* in 1938) had, during the summer timetable only, a duty which involved no less than three departures from Belfast within the space of 10½ hours. This engine had first to work the 3.30am goods to Ballymena, returning with the 7.36am passenger ex Cullybackey. 43min after arrival she was speeding to Portrush on the 9.20am Portrush Flyer, and when this crew got back to Belfast they still had to work the same engine to Whitehead at 2pm.

In the big link other departures from Belfast were the 2.40am Derry Central goods, 3.30am main-line goods, and the 6.25am and 7.25am passenger down the main line. The late turns included the 12 noon and 3.45pm passenger, the Golfers' Express and the North Atlantic Express. Tommy McClelland and Jimmy Gregg had *90* which seemed to stay on the top jobs no matter how many new moguls arrived. Known as 'Monkey', McClelland enjoyed fast running more than most and was remembered for a run in the days prior to the straightening out of loops to provide a fast road. On this occasion he ran through Glarryford in a manner which caused Sir Thomas Baird, in the dining car, to spill port over his trousers. During the war a speed restriction of 60mph was taken very seriously by the NCC right from the outbreak, but a run up from Portrush on the 6.30pm on 13 June 1943 demonstrates McClelland's method of dealing with an easy 45min non-stop timing from Ballymena. With a mere 190 tons *104* was permitted to fall below 30mph as early as Temple-patrick, though 40mph at Kingsbog showed some improve-ment. After Mossley, however, McClelland let *104* run unchecked over the viaduct at 70mph to a maximum of

75mph thus achieving a time of 43min 40sec with very little demand on the boiler.

Gregg's last year was 1948 and I clearly remember a foot-plate run with him, as senior driver, on 22 August with the 10am Sunday train to Portrush. Barely keeping time for the first 45 miles he suddenly began to hammer *101* down Ballyboyland bank to demonstrate, or so he said, how very rough she was. 75mph seemed to satisfy him and it was certainly a case of hanging on as best one could. I remember hearing that John McAllister used to test the nerve of every fresh fireman he had by trying to scare them with excessive speed approaching Bleach Green viaduct. Possibly Gregg, too, was having his little joke.

The other top-link engines during the summer of 1938 were *95, 96, 97* and *98*. It was probably typical that 'Skipper' John Young should have a new engine (*98*) which he shared with big Jimmy Marks. Young had never really outlived a holiday he had spent afloat, thereafter directing operations to his fire-man and the various shunters in the most nautical of terms. Not the most tolerant man to fire for, he had previously driven *90* for some years, taking her over Bleach Green viaduct on the occasion of its opening on 17 January 1934. He is reputed to have regularly pulled up *90* to 5% with satisfactory results, expressing the opinion that this was the only one of the moguls which suited this treatment.

Young's father had been one of the bowler-hatted brigade of drivers, another son, Stewart, sharing *96* with Bill Nixon, a quiet reliable man. Stewart Young appears to have been a 'full regulator' man also. In modern times this method found little favour with the inspector or many of the drivers, though still preached by the management who possibly remembered how much visiting Englishmen had been impressed before the war. Using extreme expansive methods must have caused additional strain in running to a class already quite rough enough.

Con McAllister had *95* and seems to have preferred a much more generous cut-off. This driver, with his quiet husky voice, had undoubtedly great standing amongst his colleagues and it is not surprising that he was the driver sent to man *96* for that week on the GNR in August 1935. His fireman during this historic visit was W.R. Wilson, an engineman who took his work very seriously and who may have been a little disappointed, in latter days, not to succeed Sam Bacon as locomotive inspector. In 1945 McAllister again figured in the news when he was selected to drive the royal train with *101*. It almost seemed like a lapse in courtesy for the royal pair in the end to decide to reach County Derry by plane, but other members of the nobility did use this train.

Jimmy Gordon, somewhat of a connoisseur on matters pertaining to alcohol, was *95*'s other driver and seems to have driven more in the modern school, midway between that of McAllister and the brothers Young. *97* was consistently in the hands of Bob McKenzie and Joe Kealy, for whom Jimmy Keenan fired. McKenzie was a red-haired man and would arrive at the shed in grand fashion with his basket, which he would hand up to his fireman.

When they had accepted the 'Derby' moguls *90-93* as remarkably good machines, the men seem then to have studied the Belfast productions with even more interest as each emerged. Thus *94*'s rather undeserved reputation as a poor engine may have been just because this was what they expected. To them the jumper blastpipe of *95* was probably just a nuisance but *96-97* seem to have been highly thought of from the first for they even had names before it was decided to call *91-95* after rivers, instead of Irish chieftains, as originally chosen. With a shorter regulator *96* and *97* seemed almost in a little class of their own, faster and not so powerful as the Derby machines.

The new batch of moguls, which began with *99*, had originally been intended to be numbered *40-45*, delivery to be completed before 1940. However, by 1938 some people were already saying that Speir had overreached himself in his expectations of traffic and that neither the Loopline nor a large fleet of moguls would ever produce an adequate return.

Many considered that even if excursion fares like 2s 6d (12½p) to Portrush and 1s (5p) to Whitehead had resulted in extra traffic it was still not economic carrying. So the mogul order was slowed up. The shops went on short time and only nine engines were repaired in 1937, the next year showing a slight improvement with eleven, but only ten were done in 1939. This compares with a year like 1943 when, despite wartime shortages, six moguls, five Whippets and no less than eight Castles were repaired at York Road.

Thus it was April 1940 before *100* (December 1938) and *101* (June 1939) were followed by *102,* still surprisingly in maroon, though repaired engines if they were now painted at all were merely given unlined black. Most of the enginemen had very definite views about the three wartime moguls. Although a boiler for *103* had been exposed to the elements at Ballyclare Junction several months before being used for this engine (presumably a cause for constant complaints during her lifetime about leaking) this mogul, which did not appear till March 1942, was the only one of the three to be in any way popular. *102* and *104* were regarded as bad steamers, though the former compensated for this in some respect by being a very fast engine.

Runs in Tables E and K with *102* and *103* demonstrate heavy loads being handled in good style for wartime conditions. They make a striking contrast, however, with another run by a new engine, *99* in Table C, which was probably rather exceptional, even for those remarkable days. 'Dicky' Rodgers had a military appearance and a slight tendency to expect his fireman to do an undue share of the donkey work, such as oiling (regular practice on the GNR). However, he enjoyed fast running and knew how to get it out of the engines. He had a respect for good timekeeping and when he thought the station time had been quite long enough he would pull the whistle. The carriages used in this run included 201/4/5 of J10, latest design, which tended to offend sensitive railway enthusiasts by having bus type seats. On this occasion *99* averaged 63mph for over 50 miles, an exceptional achievement with a heavy train over so much single line.

Fast running of this quality was best known, of course, through the North Atlantic Express. So much has already been written about this train that I can afford, space being limited, to restrict examples to runs with four different moguls, which appear in Tables B, E and I. The very conception of this train and its resultant reliable performance certainly fully justified the public's respect, though possibly few are aware that both in power and speed, mogul achievements of this pre-war period have occasionally been bettered in modern times. Even to hear a dilettante remark some thirty years after that he can still smell the bacon sizzling through the window of buffet car 90 at Portrush platform, simply reminds one of another remarkable feature.

It was only for a couple of the peak summer months that the 8.10am ex Portrush was as heavy as seven bogies, a situation which not only rather spoiled the symmetry of five carriages of similar design but made that mile a minute timing from Ballymena (fastest in Ireland at that time) impossible to keep if any kind of delay ensued. A very different type of train was the 9.45am, which combined at Antrim with carriages from Larne Harbour worked by a Castle from Greenisland. Table C shows *98* handling fourteen vehicles, making it the heaviest train of any shown in the tables.

With the last mogul, *104*, a spare mogul boiler was also delivered and this was immediately fitted to *93*, whose boiler was then given a new firebox and fitted to *92*. Thus the early moguls began to have their fireboxes renewed and by August 1946, when *95* received *97*'s reconditioned boiler, all the first eight engines had been done. A second new boiler, ordered in 1942, did not arrive till four years later, and this was given to *94*, whose boiler was in due course applied to *100*. Thus for a time two spare mogul boilers facilitated repairs until the early fifties, when the earliest ones became life expired.

Some of the mileage figures of the wartime years take some believing and it seems that the new engines, in particular, were permitted to continue in service without intermediate repair, resulting in irreparable frame damage. Two extreme cases were *102* and *104*, the former running 94,655 miles in 1945 and the last mogul achieving 88,383 miles in 1943. Dublin-Cork and back in one day is 330 miles and the GNR compounds had, during the war, a turn which produced a daily mileage of 275, but it seems very doubtful if either of these railways could claim a higher years mileage for one engine than the moguls I have mentioned. During 1946 the first seven moguls (except *94*) received overhaul at Harland & Wolff's shipbuilding yard, being transported across the Lagan, in turn, by floating crane.

Table I shows a lively run with *90*, just four months after returning from Harlands. Marshall, once attached to Carrickfergus shed, ceased express driving shortly after this run, to commence a long reign in company with another good runner, Bill Hagan, in charge of rail car 1 at Belfast. After so many years of dull stuff on the NCC with the fire seldom out of the boxes there was truly a whiff of the old days about this effort, when the Duke was the pride of York Road. The run with *92* in Table E had the same kind of pre-war liveliness with nothing very fast down the hills. The very early arrival at Coleraine (for a fast train) should be noted, the 5.10pm being due to make a crossing stop at Macfin with the 5.30pm ex Derry, but being allowed on that day as the up train was running late.

This 5.10pm was considered to be a fairly sporting train, especially when it was timed nonstop to Ballymena in 41 minutes. Apparently on one occasion a shunter at Ballymena told Keenan that there would be a 'pint' for Steenson and himself at the edge of the down platform at 5.40pm but not a minute later. It seems that both driver and fireman did assuage their thirst on this occasion, though it is rather difficult to believe that the run from Belfast was made in 30 minutes. Of a very different calibre was the run with *100* in Table E but I include it as a rare example of mogul performance during the period when this engine and *101* were fitted

F

for oil burning. John Moore was Redfern's fireman around this time, the other crew making dull runs with oil fuel being Joe Shiels and Sam Sloane.

By 1946, of course, the first four 2-6-4 tanks had arrived but even by the following June when *1-10* were all in service, there is no record of their doing anything on the mainline as good as the moguls. However, two other classes of tank engine should be mentioned, if briefly, to make the 1938-48 era's story complete.

Three 0-6-0 saddle tanks were loaned to the NCC by the GNR in 1942. Members of this LNWR design could still be seen at that period (and later) working goods and, occasionally, passenger on the Dundalk, Newry & Greenore Railway but it was not really a very inspired transfer to bring these north to the NCC, much less helpful, in fact, than the repair of five NCC locomotives at the Dundalk works. These 35 ton tanks had the same quite large driving wheels as the V class 0-6-0s. Neither did their braking power make them at all suitable for heavy goods trains so their use on the NCC seemed to be limited to shunting, for which they were nippy enough where a few wagons at a time were concerned.

The NCC career of *1, Macrory* was less than five months, due to her mechanical condition but *6, Holyhead* kept going for eighteen months, mainly in the hands of old Dan Ferguson in Coleraine, who had now come off the top jobs. It was a sure sign that dusk was coming with its resultant visual difficulties when Dan would suggest to his fireman that he might like a drive. The third engine, *4, Newry*, one of three to bear the NCC number 4A, had much the longest acquaintance, going back to Dundalk for repairs in September 1943 but returning to the NCC again in April 1944 to replace *6* and remaining till February 1946. All three engines appear to have worked a little at both Belfast and Coleraine and at the latter even performed on passenger trains occasionally, especially in the circumstances whereby the engine for Portrush arrived from Belfast in urgent need of repairs at Coleraine shed, in which case the little tank went bumping off to Portrush.

Little need be said about the two standard LMS 0-6-0 tanks of the other (Derby) breed. Once altered to the Irish gauge they were a regular sight on Belfast quays from November 1944. *19* lasted seven years after *18* was sold in July 1956.

CHAPTER 4

Halcyon Days:1949-51

In January 1948 the official name of the NCC changed from LMS (NCC) to Railway Executive (NCC), due to national-isation in Britain. With the formation of the Ulster Transport Authority in September, which included the BCDR, it seemed only a matter of time until the NCC also must be absorbed.

It is at such times that coats of arms, official colours etc assume momentary importance and J. H. Houston, in charge of York Road workshops, took this opportunity to make some enterprising experiments. If there had been any chance of retaining that unique maroon for the engines he would not have considered any other colour, but wartime conditions at York Road had finished that, apart from the three wartime moguls. Except for *101*'s repaint in 1945 for the Royal Train the only other coat of maroon paint applied to a NCC engine during the emergency had been by Dundalk, when overhauling *81*. It had been a friendly gesture.

The livery for all NCC engines was now black, lined with vermilion stripe, quite respectable and dignified, but Mr Houston decided upon a bold stroke. This new 'authority' seemed, in many respects, to be simply the Northern Ireland Road Transport Board in a different guise and their large fleet of buses had always been green. So in August 1948 the first 2-6-4 tank to be overhauled, *5,* was given a coat of apple green.

A month later the first mogul, *90*, appeared in a similar shade, which might well have reminded some of the older generation of a former GNR colour. As a contrast, *7* appeared in November in black without any lining and finally *80*, pride of Larne shed, was turned out in olive green, lined out in yellow and red. Possibly this was wrong psychology, but anyway the plan went wrong and the board decided it did not want gaily coloured steam engines.

One can imagine Mr Houston's private feelings at this period. Coming from an NCC family, and an engineer on the NCC all his life (page 36) he was now next in authority to the chief engineer, John Thompson, and could naturally expect to succeed him in due course. But NCC affairs were now to be directed from outside with the likely result that the man the UTA would appoint would certainly not be a railwayman. So indeed events proved and steam engines, as far as the authorities were concerned, passed for ever into a world of indifference and inexperience. Useful and indeed essential they would be for a time but never again would there be any pride or enterprise in steam matters from the top.

On Monday, 13 December 1948, with *104*, driver John Fitzpatrick had left Portrush at 11.35am for Belfast. At Coleraine the usual procedure was adopted of pulling forward, after which the engine with the carriages of the 11.5am from Derry went into the shed, and *104* then backed down to make the complete train. Having noted, subconsciously, that the 10.15am ex Belfast had arrived and that he should now have the single line to himself, he waited for the guard's signal to depart, just on the Belfast side of the colour light signal.

However, a section up the line, at Macfin, the daily routine had been slightly impeded by the passage of an empty carriage train from Belfast, which had been following the 10.15 all the way. Why Paddy Quinn was driving this special and not the 10.15, his rostered turn, is not clear but with fireman Tim Maguire they had been running well, Billy Hanley (at that period firing instructor) being also on the footplate. Macfin took them on from Ballymoney, as there was just a chance to squeeze them into Coleraine before the 11.5am ex Derry left there, and a Derry Central train would soon be warned on from Garvagh. So Quinn, with *93*, proceeded towards Coleraine, but a short distance outside met *104*, which had just moved off, head on, in the section.

Unable to see the signal himself and with no tablet necessary in the direction-lever section Coleraine-Macfin, Fitzpatrick, like other drivers, tended to rely on the guard's signal, but there must have been some misunderstanding, though certainly a few yards farther he would soon have come against a red advance starter. On *93*'s footplate they saw *104* coming out, but did not immediately realise that she was on the same track, so deep rooted is the railwaymen's faith in the signalling system.

Both engines and especially *93* incurred considerable cylinder and buffer damage and the front carriage of the 11.5am was derailed. No passengers were injured but both Quinn and Hanley spent several weeks in Coleraine hospital. This incident, set in the interim period after the advantages of the 'big brother' LMS had gone for ever, but before the bus-minded influence had officially commenced, seems as suitable a place as any to begin our story of how steam fared on the NCC under the UTA and its successor, Northern Ireland Railways. Only for a little more than eighteen months would the NCC continue in full spate, with engines still reaching the tip of each tentacle of the broad-gauge system.

1949

In the winter timetable, Belfast had responsibility for eight of the thirteen through mainline trains (passenger and goods). Shiels and McGonagle had *93*, Keenan and Wilson *90*, McDade and Fitzpatrick *92*, and Quinn and Cole *97*. In Coleraine, Mackarell and McAuley had *99*, Piggot and McDonald *96* and McDonnell and McClements *102*. Here *100* was spare engine. All the other moguls except *104* were either in the 'shops or waiting to enter them, apart from *95* in Derry. Names well

Page 87   BRANCH TERMINI *(above) Lisanoure Castle* at Ballyclare, 7 August 1932; *(below)* Class A1 *58*, with tender cab, on daily goods at Dungiven, 7 July 1949. Driver: J. Faulkner

Page 88   *(above)* Moneymore 17 March 1955. 10am goods ex Cookstown; *(below)* Cookstown, 5 July 1949. Class PP 4-4-0 (GNR) *106* about to depart with 4.20pm to Portadown. Carriages for 4.50pm to Coleraine in adjoining NCC station

known today can be found amongst these engines' regular firemen. Dunlop and Elliott had *96*, Houston and Coulter *102* and Doherty *95*. At Belfast McAuley was on *90*, McCracken on *92* and John Moore on *93*.

Derry, where Hinds and Wallace were the top drivers, had also three 4-4-0s, *82-4*, providing power for the 6.40am to Portrush (via Limavady) and the 7.40am passenger to Limavady. Denis McAdorey had now retired (though he lived to be over ninety) but other pre-war drivers, such as Faulkner, Neeson and McLoughlin, were finishing their days on the local jobs. Drivers at other sheds who had cleaned or fired in Derry at one time included McGonagle, Quinn, Mills, Limerick and Jimmy Simpson. Of all the Whippets in Derry at that period, *61* had been the most shining example of the cleaner's art.

Coleraine had also a working to Limavady, the 5.40am goods, this engine being responsible for working the branch and the daily goods to Dungiven. As a Coleraine engine usually worked the Draperstown goods also (after arriving with the 6.50am passenger in Magherafelt) it was desirable that three Whippets should be shedded there. The remaining members of this class, of which the last to be overhauled, *58*, was about to enter the works, were in a very rundown state, so occasionally a 'Castle' had to be used on the restricted branches. *65* and *69* had both been overhauled in 1947 but neither ran as many miles in 1949 as *62* and *64*. Cookstown and Ballymena shared this class with Coleraine, whose other 4-4-0s included *4A*, *77-8* and *85-86*.

Most of the remaining 4-4-0s were in Ballymena, where *71* and *75* each worked to both Cookstown and Belfast every weekday and *81* was almost inevitable on the 3.25pm perishable to Larne Harbour. At that period the Aldergrove train ran from Antrim to Ballymena via Randalstown, where *73* or sometimes a 'Whippet' had to run round the train. Another turn meant leaving Ballymena for Belfast with the 4.5pm passenger, and *66* could often be observed making uncertain progress with the return working, the 6.35pm ex Belfast.

When *74* came from the works in May she went to Ballymena post haste, as *33* was now barely fit to cope with even the shunting job on which she was ending her days.

The remaining class A1 engine, *34*, was regularly employed as yard shunter at York Road till September when she gave way to *66* and was withdrawn from service. Other 4-4-0s at Belfast were *70, 76* and *79,* used for ballasts and cattle specials, and Whitehead locals on Saturdays. There was also a fairly regular job for this class on the 3.55pm passenger Belfast-Magherafelt returning with the 6pm goods. This accounts for all the remaining 4-4-0s except *87,* out of use at Ballymena and *72* and *80,* still used daily by Larne.

Apart from the new tank engines, this establishes the 1949 position as regards the engines, except those which shunted only, such as *16, 18* and *19* and the three 0-6-0s *13-15,* still in original condition. Now the only engines to be seen on Carrickfergus Harbour branch, they also shunted at Belfast, with a few regular turns on stopping passenger trains, even as far as Whitehead. Larne shed and York Road each required three 2-6-4 tanks daily. One of the few turns they had on the main line involved the 8am passenger ex Cookstown and on this, on 26 January, *9* was held at Moneymore for over an hour when the blower cock joint blew out on Blackam and his fireman, Ritchie.

On 4 March *76*'s job as pilot to *71* on the 9.45am Belfast-Cookstown was not to handle fair traffic but because *69* was disabled at Magherafelt with a broken piston rod. However, *76* lost a cotter pin en route and had to be taken off at Cookstown Junction. In due course first aid was rendered here by using a wedge-shaped stick and *76* was then able to proceed to Magherafelt where a cotter was borrowed from the useless *69,* which now set off cautiously for Ballymena with her right side uncoupled. The day's entertainment was far from over, however, for a wagon had been derailed at Muckamore, leaving single line operation in force at the busiest time of the afternoon. When *81* reached Antrim from Ballymena she had the combined train of the 3.25pm perishable and the 4.5pm passenger for the crew of Gourley and Scott. *4A*, manned by Bankhead and McLoughlin, now added her weight and that of the 2.35pm ex Cookstown, the three trains combined being now worked by two engines. Thus at Cookstown Junction that day it had still been possible, within the space of a few hours, to observe an example of the three classes of 4-4-0 remaining on the NCC.

A new working timetable was issued on 7 March, which had the entire NCC and BCDR in one volume, though it was not actually until the first day of the following month that the NCC was obliged to call itself part of the UTA. This remarkable volume included about 313 miles of railway of which only 130 miles remain today.

96 had now run over 100,000 miles since last overhaul and she would continue for a couple of months yet before going to the 'shops in August when Piggot and McDonald got *98* instead. *96* would never again be shedded at Coleraine and the run in Table G does as well as any to perpetuate her spell there. 25min was an exceptionally good time to Ballymoney with a load of ten bogies and I have since wondered if, unknown to me, Piggot had got banked up the rock cutting that day, seeing the start was so brisk. This was rarely done with the 5.25, however, though it would have been quite possible for a passenger at the front of the train to be unaware of it. Table B shows an even better run of the same period, when the mercurial McDade with his faithful *92* had bettered North Atlantic schedules to Templepatrick, but eased then because he was ahead of time.

Cookstown Junction shed had been closed once again but there was an interesting arrangement to facilitate former crews, who still lived conveniently. Thus *74* would come out from Ballymena at 4.15am, work the 5.5am goods to Toome and then return from there to Randalstown to work the 6.45am passenger connection into the 6.45am ex Cullybackey at the junction. At this point one of the two local crews (J. Gilmore and T. York or H. McNally and P. Shannon) would replace the Ballymena men on *74* and work the 7.5am

passenger to Cookstown, and later the noon goods from
Magherafelt, off which they would be relieved at Cookstown
Junction by Ballymena men. The other pair took over *71* on
the 9.40am ex Belfast, arriving back with the 2.35pm ex
Cookstown and again relieved by Ballymena men.

This was the last summer in which there was a daily
through train from Larne Harbour to Derry. A tank engine
worked this 10am as far as Greenisland. Here the Coleraine
mogul off the 7.55am ex Portrush-Belfast took over (no need
for her to turn), the tank continuing into Belfast with the
vans, marshalled at the front. The reverse working, which
once had been the famous wartime 2.20pm ex Derry, lasted
considerably longer, mainly at 3.15pm. 1950 saw it worked
between Coleraine and Larne Harbour by *91*, given a summer
home at Ballymena for the purpose. On 7 July, in her absence,
73 made an unusual appearance on this important train, running the eight bogies from Coleraine to Ballymoney in a very
reasonable time of 12min 35sec though the maximum speed
was only 52mph. The down working on this turn was a local
from Ballymena to Portrush at 10.20am, which provided good
facilities for folk at rural outposts to have a day at the seaside.

Cullybackey was such a place, but to Billy Adamson it
remains the station where he and the late Christy Tracey had
their famous butter transaction. During butter rationing
Tracey and his fireman, R.J. Simpson, conceived the idea that
Adamson, who had a shop of his own in Carrickfergus, could
help out with some under-the-counter butter. The latter driver
was on good terms with a train examiner from the Antrim
area called Miller, who was able to produce some tallow from
the GNR, which Adamson neatly wrapped and labelled to
make it look like butter. He was on the 2.40am goods to
Cullybackey that week and was there waiting with the 7.20am
passenger to Belfast when Tracey arrived with the 5.55am.
The Ballymena-Cullybackey tablet was duly thrown out onto
the platform as usual and then Tracey and his fireman each
received a 'pound of butter' from their generous friend. Off
they went on the next section of their journey to Coleraine,

quite delighted with themselves, so much so in fact that they
had failed to observe that a permanent way man, assuming
the tablet he saw on the platform to be theirs, had thrown it
back onto the footplate. Thus they had two tablets and
Adamson none, so a car had to be hired to follow them to
recover the tablet.

By this period the excellent pre-war system of allocating
crews to a regular engine was being readopted and even on a
Sunday, if a crew's engine was lit up, they or their mates
expected to be in charge. Table B shows part of such a Sunday
morning run with Billy Cole. Undoubtedly this driver regarded
steam engines as almost human. It was fascinating to watch
him listening intently on the footplate, as he fiddled this way
and that to get the cut-off which sounded best. This 97
appealed to him particularly as being extremely economical
on coal and water. On this occasion when I went for a brief
word at Ballymena I found a gentleman of oriental appearance
just terminating a chat at the engine. 'I told him,' said Cole to
me with an imperceptible wink 'That I had her at 10% all the
way from Doagh.' If true on this occasion it was hardly his
usual practice though in later days, when 97 had developed
great unsteadiness on the road, it was said that this was
probably due to a spell of being pulled up too tightly.

In August 101 had a tightening up in the works and a fresh
coat of paint to go with a permanent name at last, *Lord
Masserene*, which she received officially on 8 September. This
was the last naming ceremony until the recent flash of inspiration by Northern Ireland Railways who, in 1970, revived a
number of names which had, in the past, adorned favourite
steam engines, and applied them to recent diesels. As if
speaking of some kind of unusual animal, the Railway's Chief
Executive confided to the press, as an explanation, that railway enthusiasts like to collect names.

On 5 July there had been a train-naming ceremony, with
the inauguration of the *Belfast Express* and its counterpart,
the *Derry Express*. The trains concerned were the 8.30am
and 5.30pm ex Derry and their opposites ex Belfast, the

8.25am and the 5.25pm, but there was no acceleration nor were the names very inspired, though perfectly sensible. *103* was outshopped from Harland & Wolff just in time for the first run, working right through from Derry to Belfast on this occasion. Wallace and Kerrigan were the crew as Sir Basil Macfarland, Bart, Lord Mayor of Londonderry, opened the mogul's regulator.

During May and June four more 2-6-4 tanks (*50-53*) had been received from Derby. Piggot and McDonald tried *50* for a couple of weeks while waiting for *98* to be run in but showed typical Coleraine lack of enthusiasm for this more comfortable version of their usual mount. In fact when *98* arrived from Queens Quay it was seen that Harlands had given her a resemblance to the tanks by fitting outside main steam pipes. This engine had also been given new cylinders and the original boiler off *100*, out of use since 1947 and now with a new firebox. For each of the next four years *98* was to top 50,000 miles, her crews finding her little inferior to *96*.

2 had been outshopped in April and a month later Charlie McCune was offered a newly delivered engine *52* so that *2* could go back to Larne. This canny old fellow, who refused to work in the mogul top link, would have none of the idea and *2* remained his engine until his retirement. Table D shows a mainline run with him and this engine, the earliest record I have of 80mph with this class. It also seems to have been the first occasion during which this speed had been attained on the NCC in the postwar period and, of course, before the war it was also rare, good uphill work being the main feature then.

During August *86* was overhauled, getting *85*'s boiler with new firebox. In due course her own boiler also got a new firebox and was placed in *87*, outshopped in December after two years of inactivity.

Few drivers were as steady in performance as old Pat Quinn. Most of his colleagues did not seem to realize that Paddy, muttering and chuckling through his pipe, was equal to the best of them, as exemplified in Table K. On the other hand, a man with a great reputation, Coleraine driver Davie Mackarell, rarely produced even a timekeeping run for me. On 17 February, for instance, he took 2¼min over the 41 allowance to Ballymena of the 8.25am, the fast finish there being needed after a poor minimum of 21mph with eight bogies, followed by nothing faster than 70mph. On one occasion Adamson had the brand new *10* to assist *99* to the summit and the climb was made so brilliantly that the heavily jowled Mackarell stepped off his engine at Kingsbog and up quickly onto the pilot's footplate to observe, with amazement, a full boiler of water. 'We'll have to get some of these at Coleraine,' he said, but in due course few men at that shed would ever take one if he could get a mogul. Old John McAuley crewed with Mackarell and usually kept better time, but few men cared to fire for him, a violent physical struggle being the end of McAllister's sojourn with him.

For this winter Larne had now only one 4-4-0 (*80*), for *72* had gone to Coleraine, which area had now also *76* and *79*. *83* had come up to Belfast to finish her days as spare engine. Regarded by some as the worst of her class, her final mileage was the least of all the 1924-5 engines. Most miles for the year 1949 were run by *90*. With 68,125 *102* was only 3892 less. *7* on the three crew job at Larne had 68,080 miles, the only occasions when this yearly figure has been exceeded by a tank being by *2* on the same job before *7*, and by *9* which succeeded *7*. Top 4-4-0 mileages for 1949 were by *71* at Ballymena with 50,489 and *84* at Derry with 45,967.

1950

With the withdrawal of *64* the Whippet ranks in Coleraine were thinning still further so *66* was sent there. *91* had also settled there for the winter to replace *99*. *94* was back in Derry and in February *52* was tried there also, soon to contrast sadly with the immaculate condition of sister *51* at Larne. This type, not seen regularly in Coleraine since 1947, now had a daily working on the 9.25am Belfast-Portrush.

The through goods did not stop at Ballymoney, considered important enough in its own right, apart altogether from the narrow gauge, to have its own goods trains, both from Coleraine and Ballymena. The latter left at 4.10am (the BCDR tanks had this turn for a time in 1950) the return working being the 7.57am school train to Ballymena. The four bogie set for this had arrived the previous evening on the 5.10pm ex Belfast, the 2-6-4 tank of which returned with the 9pm goods. Six years later this 7.57 had been reduced to one bogie only and shortly after was discontinued.

Ballyboyland siding was more easily served by a down train, but the more usual working was for the Coleraine engine of the local goods to propel a van with a few wagons from Ballymoney. On one occasion in the siding *72*'s tender parted from the engine, but no one was injured. On 5 June the engine was *70*, on the 2pm goods ex Coleraine, driver S. Mills. The time of this train was frequently changed to fit in with availability of engines. It was a couple of years later, after arriving at Coleraine from Limavady, that Mills again happened to be on the Ballymoney goods. In general, Coleraine drivers felt little enthusiasm for Davie Hunter's social evenings in his cottage at Damhead gates, which so preoccupied his family that they were constantly delaying trains by not having the gates open in time. So, on this occasion, finding the gate signal on yet again, Mills stopped quietly well short of the crossing and sent fireman Cameron to open the gates. When he had returned, *87*, with regulator full open and her whistle shrieking, was driven over the crossing and away towards Macfin. The lackadaisical Hunter, when he heard the engine, never thought of going outside to look but guiltily assumed the worst and phoned Macfin to the effect that the goods was running away and had smashed his gates.

The summer timetable operated from 19 June and this was to be the last year that the Derry Central alternative route could be used for Portrush trains on busy Saturday afternoons. With an optimism possibly based on the necessity of future summers, arrangements were made to ignore the Garvagh route, despite a service which included trains from Derry at 1pm and 3.15pm, from Portrush at 2.15pm, 2.30pm and 4.25pm (with a stopping railcar somewhere in the middle) against down trains from Belfast to Derry at 12.55pm and 2.55pm to Portrush at 11.55am, 1.15pm, 2.25pm and 3.25pm over the single line north of Ballymena. Most of the timings were easy enough to make the necessary strict timekeeping just possible, but the long section from Dunloy to Ballymoney meant that just one engine steaming badly was enough to upset the whole afternoon.

On 7 July Andrews wasn't having a very happy time with *93* on an empty carriage train from Coleraine. Remembering the accident there just over eighteen months previously it would seem that this engine had no luck with such workings. In any case, when he reached Ballymena the tender bearings were so warm that he took *74* instead. Later Ballymena's other McKeown, John, worked *93* up to Belfast on the 4.5pm passenger, rather a contrast to the small BCDR 4-4-2 tank normally used at this period. Even at Kellswater the box was smoking unpleasantly but McKeown worked on to Belfast. Indeed this driver seems to have thought very lightly of such matters for it was about this time that he ran *81* hot on the Sunday 2.25pm from Ballymena to Portrush. Some time afterwards a similar exploit was so much more reprehensible that John was reduced to firing and died shortly afterwards. I was sorry that this was the end of this carefree big man for he had given me some smart running with the smaller engines.

Ballymena was easily the most interesting shed at this period for at every visit they seemed to have a different selection of engines at work. The fact was that a number of NCC 4-4-0s were being run down at the same time as some BCDR engines were in use, displaced by closures there and a couple of the NCC tanks. NCC closures were also due but during the drowsy August afternoons, just prior to these, one could usually see two little County Down tanks in Antrim at about the same time.

97

230 was most often on the Aldergrove turn, which also involved shunting Muckamore yard and visiting the 'Asylum' siding. The brakes of this class were not over suitable for goods workings and during this period one of these engines got into trouble with some wagons on the steep grade between the 'Asylum' and Springfarm crossing where the small branch joined the main line. Although moving very slowly it was still not possible to prevent the engine sliding over the points onto the main line with a few wagons. Fortunately it was impossible for an up train to use the Cookstown Junction-Antrim section while the siding was in use. No one remembers exactly the number of the engine concerned. If, out of the three possibilities, it did happen to have been *213*, it is interesting to remember this engine's previous failure to control a coal train approaching Bangor.

During this period *221* appeared about twice as often as *213* on the 4.5pm Ballymena to Belfast, *74* also turning up and producing times indistinguishable from those of the little tanks. The standard allowance from Antrim to Ballyclare Junction was normally 17 minutes and in the run I include in Table L with *221* this was cut quite neatly, as was overall time to Belfast by over a minute. Very similar runs were made by several other drivers, most of whom did not seem to resent too much the extremely cramped footplate arrangements. On occasions the load was less trivial but these engines, even with four bogies, were able to keep running time, though they had nothing to spare to compensate for the frequent signal checks. One rousing effort by that extraordinary character John Orr (senior) had *213* away to 54mph by Muckamore with two bogies, but nearly 6 minutes at Templepatrick, awaiting a clear road (always a busy time on the NCC up main line) meant that despite accelerating away again to this speed before Kingsbog we took 25½ minutes to Whiteabbey. On another occasion Aaron Crowe (with Hanley aboard) allowed *221* to run to 64mph before the stop at Whiteabbey, unusually fast for this class.

A few days prior to the run with *213* I had travelled from

Antrim to Ballymena with the 4.43pm, an unusual working, being a connection to Ballymena off the 3.55pm Belfast to Cookstown. This was how the 2.35pm (ex Cookstown) engine got back to Ballymena shed each day and with four bogies 75 couldn't manage 50mph anywhere with a train which ceased to function a week later. Due at 5.1pm Jimmy Gilmore ran into Ballymena a couple of minutes down but I managed to race round to the up platform where the Larne boat train from Derry was already standing, and due out at 5pm. This had been my rather optimistic target and the log in Table L shows it was well worth the effort. *91* tended, in my view, to be the most contrary minded of the first four moguls but she seemed to be on her best steaming behaviour here. Of course engines did seem to steam well for the unscientific Dan McKeown and there must be few records of a train of this tonnage getting through Ballyclare Junction from Ballymena in under 25 minutes.

If this was haulage of a high order, I remember that summer of 1950 even more clearly for the speed exploits down Dunadry of the 9.25am to Portrush. Since the war period, speeds in excess of 70mph in Ireland had been comparatively rare so I did not really anticipate much of this particular kind of excitement from enforced daily travel to Antrim towards the end of the summer. The first week in August it was the job of Jimmy McDade with his usual engine, *92*. 28 minutes was a fair timing for a train usually made up of seven bogies and a van, and McDade was content to lose some time on this section. Indeed, the only pulse-quickening run of that first week was on the Tuesday when Billy Ritchie was doing McDade's rest day with *55* (my first run with her) and he had a maximum speed of 75mph in a time of 27min 11 sec.

From that two months' daily travel, which brought me right through this top link, some surprising speed resulted. Table A shows that most remarkable run, by the new *56*, and during that same week *97* touched 82mph in the marginally faster of two successive runs. Cole's week with this engine produced 81mph and Bob Logue, replacing W.R. Wilson, on

holiday, extracted the same maximum speed from 96. Space
permits the mention of only one other of these runs, an
occasion when Cole with 97 was piloted by 103, driven by
Bob McIlhagga (operating convenience as the load was a mere
240 tons). To my surprise the two engines, in reaching Antrim
in 25min 29sec, touched 77mph, a not altogether agreeable
thought in retrospect, considering what was to happen to two
moguls together, at speed, five years later.

In July had come the end of all traffic on the Ballyclare,
Dungiven and Draperstown branches. A month later the NCC
main line ceased to have any passenger branches, apart from
Portrush, though Magherafelt-Kilrea and the Cookstown line
continued to have a goods service. Table L shows a typical
run, out of several, with the 2.35pm ex Cookstown. All were
with 71 and none of various other Ballymena drivers, such as
Jock Orr, Bankhead or Frank Graham (junior) could get
60mph out of *Glenarm Castle*, suitably withdrawn just after
the closures.

Limavady continued to be connected with both Derry and
Coleraine by goods train. The 4-4-0 which left Coleraine for
Limavady at 6.10am continued to Derry at 10.15am, working
later the 8.10pm goods Limavady to Coleraine. The crews at
the latter were used more on the expresses now that Derry
Central commitments had ceased.

In August 102 reappeared with 98's boiler and new firebox.
The last batch of tanks had also been assembled and 55 and
56 had already shown their paces on the 9.25am to Portrush.
57 worked a coal special to Mount on 10 October and then
retired for the winter to Whitehead shed, to be joined two
days later by 101 in ex-'shops condition.

The arrival at Ballymena of 58 and 69 from Coleraine
ended the interesting use of BCDR tanks there, but 217 and
230 now saw some activity on the Larne line as well as the big
0-6-0 204 which could have been observed at Moneymore on
14 November, when 80 was derailed there with a cattle special.

1951

The New Year made its presence felt at once with such heavy snowfalls that by 3 January the automatic signalling on both shore and loop lines near Belfast was out of action. In more modern times this has been caused by thefts of copper wire and other vandalism, even railwaymen at times being suspected of being involved in this lucrative pastime. One notable raid on Greenisland booking office in 1969 meant the loss of several miles of wire and a new ticket issuing machine, all of which were carried off in one of the railway's own vans, regularly parked there during the night.

However, in 1951 the culprit was the weather and emergency telephones to assist in the flagging of trains were soon in action. Out in the country the large number of level crossings created problems and I have a note that the 8.25am to Derry, despite every effort, just managed to reach Eglinton in time to cross the 11.5am, which normally was still in Derry 25min after the down Derry Express had arrived.

Delay of another kind was experienced on 16 January when 95 reached York Road 32min late with the 3.15pm ex Derry. It had not been a lucky trip. At the outset there was serious injector trouble leaving Coleraine. Then after Ballymoney an extremely drunk passenger began to open and close the carriage doors, exposing himself to danger and generally terrifying the other passengers. The communication cord was eventually pulled near Glarryford and when the train reached Ballymena this gentleman was removed from the train to a fate of which I have no record.

Some alterations in the workings, a few weeks later, involved this important train. The engine continued to work home to Coleraine with the 9.20pm goods but the crew had to change over at the platform to a Belfast based mogul to work the 6.20pm passenger to Coleraine. That this British Railways type common-user plan did not appeal to NCC enginemen is shown by an alteration in the next timetable whereby the 6.20pm was put back to 6.35pm making it possible for the same engine to be turned and watered in time for the return trip.

Another interesting change was the reintroduction of a regular working for a 4-4-0 between Belfast and Portrush. This may have seemed like putting the clock back twenty years but the idea was quite sound and typical of Hanley, now locomotive inspector. The main passenger job at Ballymena had had its return working uprooted with the closure of the Derry Central so instead this engine, *75*, worked the 9.25am Belfast to Portrush, the second crew taking over at Ballymena. This engine then worked out of Portrush at 12.15pm and then through to Belfast again at 1.10pm, the third crew taking over at Ballymena to work out of Belfast again at 6pm. This was a very useful daily mileage of 207 and it says something for the standard of her maintenance that I very rarely saw any of the other Ballymena engines of that period (*74, 80* and *87*) take *75*'s place. Although normally at least five bogies and stopping everywhere to Portrush except Macfin and (shades of the future) Portstewart, the usual practice seems to have been to run from Belfast to Portrush on one tender of water. The regular crews of Blaney, Gilmore and McIlhagger with their firemen, Graham, York and Hamill, were experienced hands and there can have been few fireworks. During several runs I had during May, 30 minutes to Antrim was usually slightly exceeded and 64mph was the highest speed recorded.

Thinking back on this year one wonders if Major Pope's idea a few years previously of converting all tender engines into a tank version (in addition, of course, to the new tank engines just placed in service) had anything to do with the condition of the tables on this much-turntabled railway. During January both *91* and *102* became derailed on the modern Belfast one, and the Portrush table put in her periodical claim with a similar accident to *90* in April. Another feature of NCC operations had been the fitting of tablet catchers so that trains passing block stations on the fast road could do so at 70mph. Should an engine get badly down on her springs or suffer severe damage the catcher she carried could be a few inches out with the instrument on the lineside, resulting in failure to collect the tablet at the point of contact. This was tested regularly and especially before important traffic operations. On 16 March *93* was entering the coal yard at Derry when she knocked off her tablet catcher. Later she had to work the 3.15pm forward from Coleraine without one, but only 3 minutes were lost to Belfast using handloops throughout. In modern times this has had to be resorted to on every occasion, with the engine crews well aware that no one at the top knows or cares about this situation. 1950 was very different however and Inspector Hanley and that rotund ruddy little man, Inspector Tom Rainey, discussed every possibility (for the sake of those few minutes), including borrowing from *95*, also at the shed.

On 10 March *85* was in trouble on the 4.15am goods Cookstown Junction to Kilrea. For some unexplained reason the water was allowed to get so low in the boiler by the fireman that the back lead plug melted after Upperlands. This was the occasion when John McKeown decided to go on instead of dropping the fire and the damage to *85* was so considerable that she had to go into the works. Apparently even by 1951 these York Road workshops had not got used to tank engines, for *52* had to be returned after overhaul because she was sent out without a heating connection at the chimney end (for bunker first working).

This was the year of the Festival of Britain and a sign that the NCC still had some pride was evidenced by a new Festival Express (page 123) which appeared in May between Derry and Belfast. This was simply the old 8.30am ex Derry, returning from Belfast at 5.25pm, but as the latter had begun to include a stop at Antrim the standard of running required to keep the 2¼ hour timing was probably the highest since prewar days. One of the most satisfactory aspects of all this was the construction of no less than eighteen new coaches, in addition to a new dining car (87) which had appeared a short time previously.

Two of the new carriages were remarkable in being compartment stock, presumably as a gesture to Bangor line services, and *351* and *361* were easily the last of this type to appear on the railways of the north. The sixteen corridor coaches were of four types, capable of making up two splendid mainline trains daily in each direction. *301-6* were side corridor thirds while *321-6* were also thirds but of vestibule type, something the NCC came to lack more and more as *201-9* were at that time being converted into diesels and the war had taken its toll of the superb J4 and J5 type, dating back to pre-mogul days. *341* was a 1st/2nd compo and *342* a 1st/3rd compo, both side corridor, of course. The list is completed with *331-2* both brake thirds, side corridor.

In the Festival train both Derry and Portrush portions had one of the brake thirds, the other two Portrush coaches being a corridor third (J16) and the 1st/3rd compo 342 (F7). Apart from the dining car and the brake third, the three other Derry carriages were a corridor third, a vestibule third (J17) and the other compo to give superior accommodation. As the other thirds were completed they helped to make the 8.25am a better looking train and were also useful to strengthen the 5.25pm as required.

All these carriages had the edge even on 'North Atlantic' coaches 91-4 as regards smooth running, with the additional advantage of proper ventilation, a sore point with the latter vehicles. I particularly remember 324, the third coach of the 5.25pm over a long period, and undoubtedly the carriage in which I have travelled most miles at 80mph. This became MPD No 40 in rebuilt form and nine other diesel units has been the ultimate fate of more of these carriages. The other six (301-6) still retain some vestige of their original gentlemanly status by being hauled about to this day, in the form of diesel trailers 529-34.

I tried out the 5.25pm three times that May and the magnificence of the new carriages and Guard Jack Sloane's new bow-tie could not quite compensate for Johnny McAuley's failure on each occasion to keep the difficult

Page 105   PORTRUSH *(above)* 80 *Dunseverick Castle* leaving with
return excursion on a July evening in 1952; *(below)* Six 2-6-4
tanks setting off for Coleraine after arriving with excursions on
a July Saturday in 1954. Engines, in order, *54, 7, 2, 56, 57, 50*

Page 106   (above) 52 at Portrush with steam crane for 104, derailed the previous afternoon, 2 August 1958. 74 at turntable; (below) Bob Bowman (Foreman at Portrush) handing tablet to footplate crew of 2-6-4T 6 driver R. Graham and fireman T. McCrum, at Portstewart, June 1965

27min booking to Antrim. *101* was usually a better engine on the banks than *99* and had no trouble some months later (Table A) with this timing. During 1952-3 much faster running, though not stronger pulling than McDonald's, was repeatedly experienced with this splendid express.

An apt job for a stranger to the NCC main line on 15 May was the transfer from winter hibernation at Ballyclare Junction of a set of BCDR coaches, by *208* to Antrim. On 8 June *56* went to Ballymena to haul up *221*, which was able to register some shunting mileage in York Road goods yard when suitable trimmings had been applied to the boxes.

That excursion traffic to Whitehead had not entirely ceased, since the legendary sixpenny trips of Speir's day, was demonstrated on 13 July when *53* worked a Sunday School special over a route which involved such interesting track as Randalstown–Cookstown Junction and Monkstown–Greenisland. More important was the Apprentice Boys' traffic, a few weeks later. Yet four specials, hauled by *91, 92, 94* and *99*, were to be doubled in the sixties.

In modern times the invariable motive power for a batch of NCC specials was the 2-6-4 tank. Quite an early example of this occurred on another important Ulster occasion, 'Black Saturday', when the men of the Royal Black Preceptory parade at various points. On 25 August, the month's last Saturday, the venue was Ballymoney and three of the specials came from the GNR, being taken over at Antrim by NCC tank engines. The firemen involved this day provide a remarkable forecast of stirring events of the late sixties, when these three young men would all graduate to be driving tank-hauled specials. R.J. Simpson was firing to Charlie McCune on *2*, Paddy Dobbin to James Fitzpatrick on *5*, and Willie Gillespie to Billy Adamson on *52*.

When the Ballymena railcar (4) was unfit, for once, to work the 12.45pm ex Belfast on 21 September, Blaney can hardly have been delighted to get the BCDR 'Baltic' for the job. With fireman Savage he apparently lost 6min going down and Boden, on the return trip, lost 8min. However, it should be remembered that these early NCC railcars were sharply timed, if the conditional stops were made, and Table L does show *222* doing rather better. Boden, like his mate McNinch at Ballymena, was nearing retirement so possibly did not welcome a strange engine, normally used on a short 12¼ mile line. Twenty years later both men and Blaney, with a total of over 240 years between them, were still alive. A further example of antiquity was evident in one of the two carriages used in Limerick's run with *222* (page 124). This was 80, one of two old 'halt' coaches, formerly part of a rail-motor and later used in a set of carriages which also included the three ex-DNGR six-wheelers, 97-9.

The winter timetable, from 24 September, had one new working, which though railcar was interesting as providing a Mondays-Thursdays passenger service over the 'back line'. This was the 6pm ex Kilroot, which ran to Belfast via Ballyclare Junction to give Courtaulds workers a service to mainline stations. The 6.35pm local Belfast–Ballymena had been withdrawn, so the 6.20pm to Derry made the Ballyclare Junction and Doagh stops.

14 had come from the 'shops in September, rebuilt with a 'Whippet' boiler, one of the 200lb pressure variety, originally carried by *58* but then passed to *24* in 1945. With regional thriftiness the NCC usually made use of every possible asset and the workshops must have been wondering since 1947 what they could possibly do with a firebox used for only 75,000 miles. So *14* got a new lease of life and, indeed, a new look, and in a postwar NCC so dominated by engines of mogul type, those who like the unusual settled on this rebuilding as the only tolerable aspect of the modern NCC. The authorities seemed quite interested too and a number of test runs were made with goods trains on the banks. Some footplatemen, with little knowledge of the 'Whippet' type, had experiences of poor steaming with this class, now known as V1, so reception by the crews was rather mixed.

The run with the gnome-like Hughie McDonnell in Table B represents about the best down run of ten days continuous winter travel with the 8.25am. 'The Stallion' was a strong but rather temperamental engine for steaming, especially as originally built with jumper blastpipe and large chimney. *91* had somewhat the same tendency but an up run with Quinn in the same month, with eight bogies, included a superb climb (Antrim-Ballyclare Junction in 11min 11sec), a contrast to *90*, now on her last legs on Ballymena locals

CHAPTER 5

The Great Mogul:1952-4

During this chapter the first six moguls reach their twentieth birthday, with only one casualty. Before the war, though brilliant in performance and extremely important to the operations, they were numerically less than either the Castles or the Whippets (classes A1 and B3 combined). Now they really dominate the main line, though still numerically below another class (the 2- 6- 4 tanks).

1952

If the New Year of 1951 had been introduced in the trouble-some note of heavy snowfalls and signal failures, the first incident of this year that I have noted is of a lighter nature, causing no doubt many a chuckle over the enginemen's grapevine. Albert Swann, large and faithful fireman of driver Sammy Hayes, was in trouble with the stationmaster at Antrim. That gentleman, having apparently taken the trouble to cross the footbridge to greet the 7.55am ex Portrush, had complained that he had been soaked to the skin by water from *98*, presumably from the spray for water-ing the coal.

   Ballymena had provided most valuable repair facilities during the war and even at this stage was handling quite a few of the less complicated jobs. In January *54* was in with a hot box (a rare complaint for this type) and then *92* arrived under her own steam with a badly cracked framing, a serious problem with even the later moguls by this time. John Wilson and fireman McNabb, on their way back with *54*, stopped at Cookstown Junction to attach *104*, about which a decision concerning heavy repair had now been made.

84 was still a regular performer on the 1.10pm ex Derry and on 28 February the heavy 3.15pm, in addition, was powered by a four coupled engine, when *79* had to be taken off the shunting duty to replace *53*, with a faulty smokebox door. *79* slipped very badly getting away with the seven carriages. Another 4-4-0 replacement occurred on 16 May when *98* had to be removed at Ballymena from the 7.55am ex Portrush, with a bad knock in the left small end. Hayes took over *86* for the remainder of the run up to Belfast. *80* had also helped to provide an unusual spectacle on 16 April when she piloted *99* on the 8.25am Derry train, her derailment on Antrim turntable just after midnight on 29 January being, in fact, a less exceptional incident. A more unusual casualty on 21 April was one of the old horses, which before the present motorway activity in the area could usually be seen ending their days on the reclaimed land (Port Arthur) near the first milepost. The engine responsible was *1*, working into Belfast with the 4.5pm ex Larne.

With the end of the passenger service on the Limavady branch *58* had been transferred from Coleraine to Ballymena. For much of the early part of the year she worked on the turn whereby an engine shunted at Antrim and Muckamore during the afternoon before going to Aldergrove for the workers' train to Ballymena. Though no longer with the 200lb pressure boiler and now with the *24*'s tender, *58* with double exhaust valves like *33* and *69* was still regarded as a good engine. Although not officially withdrawn till April 1954, she did not run after the summer of 1952 and finished with 642,370 miles in her rebuilt state, amongst the highest of the class, though the last to be 'built'.

An even more interesting engine to observe working through Antrim (NCC) at this time was GNR 4-4-2 tank *187*, which worked out from York Road to Cookstown Junction and back with the 5.38pm on 16 May. Inspector W. Hanley had with him on the engine fireman Cole and driver Mahon, the latter far from pleased with the lively springing. On the down trip *187* kept time without trouble, reaching 56mph in a smart start to stop time of 4min 43sec from Doagh to Templepatrick. The log of the return trip is given in full in Table J. As the BCDR tanks had by now departed, this seems likely to have been the last service train on the NCC main line worked by a four coupled tank.

Plans for the summer became evident earlier than usual this year with *102* emerging from Cookstown Junction storage on 28 April and *6* from Whitehead two days later, both in ex-'shops condition. *97* remained quiescent in Whitehead till 12 June, despite the fact that on 1 May *81* was transferred to the GNR at a fee of £30 per week, to be followed a fortnight later by *57*. May produced some excellent running, especially by *102* (Tables A and D). Her hibernation had certainly done her no harm.

From the same month and Table K comes a run with *73*, one of her many appearances on this train during this period. During her fairly short life in rebuilt form (page 35 shows how she looked prior to that) this well thought of engine worked either from Larne or (consistently for her last ten years) Ballymena.

During June *103* developed a bad crack in her framing. In addition she became extremely rough riding and drivers were instructed not to pull her up, but to use the small valve with the lever well out. On 16 June *98* arrived at Belfast with a broken spring, working the 1.10pm ex Derry. Ten days later I had the run with her shown in Table G, included mainly because of the high average speed for a short distance (52½ mph) and the unusual arrangement for a scheduled Derry train to be calling at minor stations like Ballyclare Junction and Doagh, due in fact, to the withdrawal of the 6.35pm local

112

train. After Antrim *98* showed little inclination to hurry.

The 1952 summer timetable came in with the mogul situation at Coleraine in a critical state. Normally most of the big tendered engines (*99-104*) were shedded there but from time to time some of the older moguls, especially *91, 95* and *96*, had also had long and successful spells with certain crews. With *99* and *100* coming from the 'shops in March and *102* in mint condition, stored at Cookstown Junction, everything seemed at first well organised, as usual. But when the senior driver at Belfast, Joe Shiels, had his engine (*91*) put into the 'shops in March he got *100* in her place and held onto this engine throughout the summer. Then the condition of *103* became so serious in June that she had to be taken out of service, *101* was still in the works and *104* semi-derelict for nearly two years. *94* and *95*, at Coleraine all winter, had now a high mileage and were not fit for daily heavy work. *98* was not much better. Thus when *97* came out of store at Whitehead, where she was being kept for the extra Belfast jobs in the summer timetable, she had to be sent instead to Coleraine, possibly for the first time in her history.

On 18 June I observed this fast and economical engine go out on the 8.25am and I wondered how she would stand up to the thrashing invariably required for this tightly timed train in the summer when it was heavy. So I enquired of her driver, Billy Piggot, the next day how he had fared and that volatile little man, whose fireman had once thrown his shovel right into the firebox in disgust at so much nagging, looked more grim than usual. She had, he said, primed so badly that they had taken 21 minutes to Ballyclare Junction. A slight smile followed as he added that a further 22 minutes (for 22¾ miles) had seen them stopped at Ballymena. This was the beginning of a battle which ensued for nearly a month, one in which I felt almost personally involved, this engine for some years being a special favourite. When eventually they did get her to steam a mysterious knock developed and Mr Houston and other executives were asked to make footplate trips in an attempt to have them convinced that the engine was probably as unsafe as she was rough riding. On 29 July there was more bad priming on the 8.25am and R.J. McCahon, with fireman Elliott doing everything he knew, took 24 minutes to pass Ballyclare Junction with ten bogies. Later in Portrush, *94* arrived on the 9.25am with bad injector trouble, so driver Mahon was looking for another engine. Not surprisingly Coleraine promptly offered him *97*, no doubt with tongue in cheek, but the inspector saw that that shed got her back again almost at once. He did not intend to lose this battle with Coleraine's top drivers, even if they had a few years on him in actual length of service.

By this time the authorities had probably little doubt that the inevitable condition of the moguls was such that only extreme dedication could keep them going on this kind of work much longer. If these old drivers had been more amenable to accepting the tanks instead, there was some kind of solution there, but like the GNR men some years later they were not happy with them on ten bogie trains on the banks and especially with their braking potential on goods trains. So an expedient which became almost daily practice this summer was the banking of the 8.25am out of Ballymena, the 4-4-0 (usually *77*) dropping off just before Galgorm gates.

It is not altogether so untypical of the NCC that, despite carefully prepared plans for efficient working of the Apprentice Boys specials to Derry on 9 August, considerable delays should in the end ensue due to a broken tablet catcher at Killagan and that this should have been caused by empty carriages going up the previous evening to form one of the specials. The most interesting special this year was from Ballymena because it gave one the rare spectacle of driver McNinch on a steam engine (*7*) instead of his usual railcar. The family name was well-known in the north during the thirties because of a redoubtable soccer fullback of massive proportions, and Billy McNinch himself was an important member of the local (Ballymena) council. An interesting feature of this return trip was that *7* continued forward to

Randalstown with the first three bogies.

A week later the footplate combination of Ned Curran and Joe Nutt at Derry was in some trouble for permitting the water to get below the safety level on *84*, resulting in damage to the crown of the firebox. This was with the so-called 'perishable' 6.5pm Derry to Ballymoney, which they were booked to work as far as Eglinton only. This train was a short-lived episode in the gradual withdrawal of services from Waterside.

Autumn days saw York Road 'shops repair *96, 8, 74, 101, 104, 95* and *53* with commendable speed, *74* being noted on test on the triangle formed by the 'back line', a useful spot to stop to feel the boxes without holding up other traffic. The most interesting job was *104*, now rebuilt with outside steam pipes and new cylinders. In addition she had received the boiler off *102* with reconditioned firebox, which was to serve her till the end of her days. No doubt it was the sorry state of *103*'s frames which motivated this decision as she seemed always a more lively engine and would normally have been better entitled to a change of boiler. Even this new looking *104* failed to steam satisfactorily for the Coleraine men, until Hanley had the blastpipe orifice altered from $4\frac{3}{4}$ in to $4\frac{5}{8}$ in.

97 had ended her inglorious summer at Coleraine and was booked for another winter of hibernation. On her way to Whitehead she hauled *91*, also for storage. That other refuge, Cookstown Junction, was in the news on 25 November when *4*, now shedded at Ballymena, headed a cortège which had been occupying a siding there for some time. *62, 69* and *230* were placed inside the forty-one-year-old shed, with *213* outside.

The winter timetable showed some retrenchment. Instead of running the afternoon perishable from Ballymena, the 1.10pm ex Derry was booked to call at Ballyclare Junction. Here the vans were detached to be worked by another engine to Larne Harbour. At the Derry end Ballykelly and Carrichue ceased at last to have a public service. For some years their only train had been the 6.55am ex Derry, altered now to 7am, with an unadvertised call at Carrichue only. Whitehouse was still open and all the other mainline stations except Mossley and Macfin. Muckamore's sole passenger service in the up direction was now by the 7.20am ex Cullybackey but there were three possibilities in the down. Other economies included cutting back the 9.25am ex Belfast to Ballymena (instead of Portrush) and the discontinuance of the two late night goods, 9pm ex Coleraine and 9.20pm ex Belfast.

For a complete picture of the locomotive workings in 1952 the reader is advised to refer to the separately published pamplet. This particular year is selected as giving the most balanced and typical picture of the postwar steam NCC, with no foreign engines in use and just before the introduction of the first multiple unit diesels. The minimum daily mileage was then about 4500. Having digested the details I doubt if many will agree with a comment of the late George B. Howden of the GNR when I referred to the comparative efficiency of the (rival) NCC. 'They are a small concern,' he retorted. 'It is very easy for them.'

1953

The Christmas period had passed uneventfully and indeed the last incident of note had been as far back as 17 November, when *87* lost a tyre between Castlerock and Coleraine when working the 1.10pm ex Derry. The next mishap was on 15 January when driver Bankhead managed to derail *77* at Glarryford when shunting with the 3.50am goods ex Ballymena.

One of the most important aspects of this year was that no less than six of the smaller engines were reboiled within the space of ten months. Apart from *14*'s rebuilding in 1951, it was six years since a G6 (Whippet) boiler had gone into an engine and four years since the larger G7 boiler had been renewed in a repaired engine, so this was a reversal of policy indeed when interest seemed to have been mainly in the possibility of multiple unit diesels. Two G7 boilers to be fitted in due course to *75* (March 1953) and *76* (October

1953) were interesting in that they were off *Glendun* and *Glenaan* respectively, withdrawn 1946-7. The boiler off *2* had originally come new from Scotland with *83* and the firebox was apparently still good enough for use in *75* until that engine was withdrawn over three years later in June 1956. *3*'s boiler had been fitted new in 1926 and lasted throughout her career as class U1. A new firebox was now required (mileage 497,791) and this was fitted in March 1952 so that the boiler was waiting for the next Castle to go in, *76*.

The G7A boilers with wide firebox had been taken out of *86* and *87* in 1949 and these were now given new fireboxes and fitted to *78* (May 1953) and *72* (December 1953). The other two reboilerings were even more interesting, for *14*'s sisters were now similarly rebuilt as class V1. *13* got the 200lb pressure boiler formerly in *69* in February and *15* got a similar boiler from *60* in December. Thus there was more boiler work done on the engines in 1953 than during the whole ten years after. Fortunately for the modern enthusiast, however, even this activity was exceeded during 1964-5 when no less than eight of the tanks received new fireboxes.

It was anticipated that a royal train would be required in July and preparations began as early as 30 March. Two of the many 'Jimmys' at York Road (Mallon and Simpson) worked *100* to Adelaide, where two more NCC enginemen took her over. They were the senior driver Joe Shiels and his fireman Percy Mitchell. Most enginemen would welcome an honour such as this and it is of intriguing interest that in September 1971, when Joe Shiels was finally laid to rest in Milltown cemetery, Belfast, his age was stated to have been eighty-five, in which case he should really have been retired in 1953.

Queen Elizabeth was now shedded at Coleraine but she had a most apt regal title and indeed had been Shiels's engine during much of 1952. The idea now was a test run from Adelaide (GNR) to Derry (Waterside) on the timings planned for the royal visit. In 1945 *99* had been in too poor repair to haul the king during his visit to Northern Ireland, so that *101* had deputised and carried *99*'s plates *King George VI*. Here again, if *100* had any **particular** desire to haul royalty she was foiled in the end for *102* was the eventual engine. There is no doubt in my own mind that the most exceptional running during the twelve months prior to the royal visit was that performed by these two engines, but it may just be a coincidence that the authorities seemed to take a similar view by involving them directly or otherwise with this royal train.

It was March when I began to sample *100* in her best form, for it must be said that over previous years this engine had made no particular impact. Tables A and C detail only a few of a score of magnificent runs with this mogul during April and May. Apart from those shown, Robbie Miller with *100* stopped in Antrim in 27½min with ten bogies and in another Fillis touched 84mph. Every Coleraine driver seemed to have success with this engine and on the very few occasions when *91, 97,* or *98* deputised on that 5.25pm the work was less lively. However, Table A does include a run with *104*, just to show her in brighter than usual form.

So 1953 was a notable year in many respects though sometimes things did go wrong. On Saturday, 23 May, for instance, *96* went out of Belfast with a 10.45am special to Portrush and 10 minutes later was sitting on Bleach Green viaduct with cracked cylinder and smashed cylinder cover. *92* went to her rescue, shunting the disabled engine off the mainline at Monkstown. *96* was about due for the works in any case, which had just turned out the last BCDR engine in use, *229*, which went back to Queens Quay for a time. The 'shops also repaired *102* in April but took her in again towards the end of June, when *86* was outshopped, for an even more splendid coat of paint.

The final test for the royal occasion took place on 1 July when *102* worked the ten coach train of assorted vehicles to Portadown and back, from Great Victoria Street. The ex North Atlantic Express buffet car 90 rather let the NCC down by developing a hot box and was left behind at Lisburn on the return trip. On 3 July the royal party arrived in Derry before time and everything went without a hitch. In addition to the usual pilot preceding the royal train, it was thought advisable in the unsettled times to have an additional pilot in advance of *86*, and this was performed by *56*, three different classes being thus on view in the unlikely event of the monarch being interested. The pilot drivers were the other most senior men at York Road, Bill Hagan and W.R. Wilson.

The previous day children from all parts of the province had been transported to Balmoral to see the Queen. To this the NCC made its contribution with five specials: *53* from Kilrea, *80* from Dunloy, *91* from Limavady, *97* from Portrush and *98* from Larne. The GNR handled the Cookstown contingent as well as specials from Strabane and Derry. It should be remembered that on this same day two NCC engines were still on loan to the GNR, *57* working the 1.30pm to Warrenpoint and *81* the 3.10pm to Clones. So within twenty-four hours ten shining NCC locomotives could have been observed at Adelaide, no one anticipating, at that time, that around 1963 something of the kind would be quite a common phenomenon, except, of course, in the matter of cleanliness.

Other 1953 runs appear in Tables E,H,J, and N. Three of these were with mainline expresses and include that exciting exit from Derry alongside the Foyle, where an immediate impression of great haste is easily explained when we realise that there is only one other city terminus in Ireland from which in under 10 minutes from the start the speed is likely to exceed 60mph, the GNR one from Amiens Street, Dublin. The other run had exceptional interest in that mogul, *97*, had to be replaced by a 4-4-0 at Ballymena.

Nowadays requirements off the steamers at Belfast for the main line, even in the summer, are easily satisfied by a diesel train with less than 300 passengers, but the fifties usually demanded an 8.25am of ten bogies or more and to avoid a duplicate, piloting to Kingsbog summit had frequently to be resorted to. During the sixties a train headed by two 2-6-4 tanks was not unusual but more impressive in 1953 was a brace of moguls in full cry. On 27 July *102* was piloting *91* on the 8.25am and two days later the combination was *97* piloting *104*. *97* was still far from satisfactory, with a cracked framing and neither injector working properly. The two new men in the top link at Belfast, Billy Adamson and Bob McKeown, had many a struggle with her when no other engine was available.

The usual 'demonstration' specials were principally composed now of ex-BCDR six wheelers. On 29 August Royal Black Preceptory specials brought more NCC specials onto the GNR, and I have a note of five passing through Antrim in fairly quick succession: McClements of Coleraine had *74*, Downey of Ballymena had *78*, Meneilly of Larne *51*, and Belfast drivers W.R. Wilson and W. Kerr *53* and *4* respectively.

An unusual phonecall received at York Road this summer was from the driver of *85*, complaining that her whistle had stuck. Certainly a few seconds of the piercing NCC whistle is long enough. For many years a feature of NCC expresses was the habit of many of the older drivers of causing an echoing effect when whistling. In a mogul the whistle was just out of reach of a driver when he was seated, so he usually had a wire attached for his convenience and when this was let go suddenly it produced that very individual sound.

By now *70* and *82* had made their last revenue-earning runs and on 17 October *96*, running in after 'shopping, hauled them from Belfast to Greenisland, where they occupied an exposed position in a siding for a long period. *7* returned from the Bangor line a week later, making the penultimate passage of this class over the Lagan bridge. More tidying up occurred a few weeks later when *100* worked a train of empty cattle wagons to Ballymoney, continuing light to Coleraine, where the crew changed to *84*, due in Belfast for shopping. *Lisanoure Castle* was always rather a favourite with the locomotive inspector and she was to be repaired yet again in 1956.

79's future was less secure, for her boiler was life expired. On 14 October she had departed before dawn for the Derry Central with a big train of empty cattle wagons. Progress had not been good. Indeed, it rarely is on this kind of operation, for unless there is a firm hand about, the unwritten law is to extract some overtime if possible. However, in this case there did seem some justification for delay as a rivet had blown out of the firebox plate, with 79 progressed only as far as Randalstown. No doubt both Belfast and Magherafelt (where the goods was) were considered for assistance but in fact it was Ballymena which sent along 73. In due course this engine made a good run to Kilrea, returning with thirty-five loaded wagons. At Randalstown 79 was also attached and the cavalcade rolled into Belfast at about 7.30pm. This was not quite *Kenbaan Castle*'s last run for I had a few trips with her on Larne trains in December, but it seems likely that it was her last day in the country.

There were now two tanks in Derry, 50 and 55, with 74 and 75 alternating on the 1.10pm job. Troubles rarely come singly, for after some wagons had been derailed at Lisahally (fireman Joe Nutt was blamed) Sammy Miller crashed through Umbra gates the following morning with the 8.30am ex Derry. The view from an up train of the signal here and the amount of time then left for action had long been a major topic of conversation on the Londonderry and Coleraine.

It was about this time that Coleraine's '24 hour' fitter, James Markland, did a good job on 75's boxes. Every Friday being pay day the Refreshment Room at Coleraine was swarming with railwaymen in the late afternoon and on this particular occasion they were expecting Markland to pay his usual call. The two popular girls in the bar, Gráinne and Nancy, had a fine understanding of how railwaymen tick, including the need for facilities for backing horses. The organised job this day, however, required more a sense of timing than anything, as 75 clanked slowly down through the station prior to working the 5.25pm ex Belfast forward to Derry. One of the girls brought the crowded bar to a deathly hush as she announced 'Shush! Listen to that engine! Did you ever hear anything as bad as those big ends?' It was very fortunate that a roar of laughter succeeded in drowning Markland's surprised response.

1954

The new year found *5* at Derry in place of *50*, an engine no shed seemed anxious to retain very long. On 29 January, with driver Wallace on the 3.15pm ex Derry, *5* broke a piston head near Eglinton. This delay meant that *99*, due to work the train forward from Coleraine, could not be in Belfast in time to return with the 6.25pm. A van with a relief Belfast crew was therefore sent to Ballyclare Junction, where both trains were booked to stop. Here they took over the 3.15pm, thus enabling the Coleraine men to take over the 6.25pm from there. This kind of high quality operating to avoid delay to passengers is certainly a contrast to the average railway practice today.

On 13 January *99* **had** incurred the ire of the RAF at Ballykelly. In course of working the 11.15am ex Derry she had smashed into one of their lorries whilst crossing the airfield. A fortnight later an RAF officer held a session of inquiry with driver Brangam and his fireman W.J. McCahon. Yet another mishap on the Derry section occurred on 30 January when *102* broke a piston head with Piggot, when working the 5.40am goods ex Coleraine.

Not so long before, the NCC had a strong complement of plump, fleshy drivers such as Davie Mackarell, but now they had no one to compare with Hammie Macnamara, transferred from the Bangor section during January. Once up on the footplate it was quite a job for him to extricate himself again and his fireman tended to have an anxious time. His first duty on 8 January was to bring back *10* the last steam engine (apart from *229*) to the NCC from Queens Quay.

During the early part of the winter Whitehead shed had been unusually empty but at the end of the year *101*, run in after 'shopping, was stabled there, being joined on 16 February by *103*, in similar condition. It was about this time that an economy measure was first tried, to reduce the cost of washing out boilers. Certain engines were selected to have their boilers treated with a substance called Botan, which was

Page 123   NAMED EXPRESSES *(above)* Derry Express passing Ballyclare
Junction 18 August 1955 with *91 The Bush.* (5.25pm ex
Belfast); *(below)* Festival Express at Ballymoney with *101
Lord Masserene*, 3 September 1951. Driver W. McDonald
and fireman F. Dunlop

Page 124 (above) The un-named 'Scotch' engine at Garvagh, 26 August
1950, with 5.35pm ex Portrush; (below) Ex-BCDR 4-6-4T
222 about to leave Cookstown Junction with 7pm to Belfast,
6 September 1951

put into the boiler through the **left** injector. *101*, when she
went into traffic again, was one of those so treated over a
lengthy period, others being *8* at Larne and *54* at Belfast.
Many a bitter word came from the firemen concerned and
when one of these engines was observed down at the ash
dump blowing off steam in regrettable fashion it was almost
certainly an attempt to get rid of a recent dose of Botan. The
locomotive inspector had the job of converting the men to
the new system and on many footplate trips used his experience to demonstrate that adequate steam could be raised in
the victimised engines.

More intelligent control work occurred on 6 March when
a big football special to Derry had *97* piloting *96*. This train was
stopped at Glarryford by signal, and driver Ned Nelson
instructed to return with *97* to Ballymena, where *91*, on the
ordinary 10.25am, had insufficient steam to tackle the bank.
Considering the small gap between the two trains this must
have been a spontaneous decision. March is traditionally the
time of the year for important football matches and the
following Thursday, to accommodate Derry supporters
returning from a replay at Bangor, the 5.25pm had to be
strengthened to eleven carriages, *6* piloting *91* as far as Kingsbog Junction.

Early in March *81* returned from the GNR. Most of her
time had been spent on the easy Clones schedules but her very
consistent appearance certainly suggested reliability, even if
the quality of the running was barely average. *73* emerged
from York Road 'shops a few days later and may well have
been intended to replace *81* but before she could be run in *72*
was sent instead, Sam McCready, who already had Hanley's
approval for his handling of NCC engines, working her from
Antrim to Adelaide.

But Derry was in the football news again on 27 March.
Derry City's success in the Irish Cup seems to be always very
important to NCC men, even when they live in Belfast, and
locomotive plans were laid well in advance. *56* had worked
through to Derry on 19 March on the 11.10am, certainly at

that time a very unusual engine to be seen west of Coleraine. This was possibly a natural distrust of both *5* and *55*, either of which might disgrace the shed on the big day. On the same day *95* emerged from the 'shops and the following Wednesday this engine, too reached Derry on the 11.10am. Satisfaction was expressed on this occasion about her ex-works condition. The Saturday morning activities began modestly with *75* on the 7am to Coleraine. *91*, only just lit up in time as the cleaners had been engaged all night on her tubes, worked out the ordinary 8.30am express, *95* proceeding her with an 8.10am football special. In the meantime *104* had arrived with empty carriages and this engine had the 9.45am special to Belfast, *56* hauling the last special at 10.45am.

On 20 April, *99*, now also ex-works, had a Linfield football special to Derry. With *101* and *103* brought out of Whitehead for the Easter extra traffic the mogul position seemed a great improvement on the previous year. Traffic was exceptionally heavy on 21 April and a twelve-coach 8.25am had to have yet another carriage added at Ballymena. Brangam with *102* doubtless felt he deserved a good mark for being only 3min late into Coleraine with this load, but he had *52* piloting the entire trip, driver J. Bell. On 23 April *102* again had a pilot right through to Coleraine on the 8.25am. *101* came off there and returned to Belfast hauling *74* requiring overhaul. The Irish Cup Final had to be replayed that year, on Thursday, 29 April, and for this a thirteen carriage special left Derry at 3.45pm with *101*. It is difficult to imagine Johnny Kelly getting a swing on with a train of this size but it seems that he lost no time.

Over the years most enginemen regarded *78* as an excellent engine and the fact that she ran so long with the wide firebox may have helped steaming. A run with this engine on the major Ballymena train for home-bound commuters is shown in Table D. Old John Orr (page 36) was only one of several eccentrics at Ballymena shed. That capable but uncompromising driver, Sam Blair, used to exhibit unexpected possibilities of humour beneath his ruddy countenance when handing over

an engine to Orr. Jock would be told to look out for this and
that which might give trouble and he would be fussing about
anxiously for the rest of the trip with that huge oilcan.
Normally Orr worked an engine extremely hard, not from any
pleasure swift movement gave him, but from over-anxiety
about timekeeping. When he got an engine of power class E
with a light load, some of the unnecessary lashing he would
give her produced for me, at any rate, some remarkable
sectional times. However, in this example, the average
Braidman's partiality for the 'Scotch' engines is shown by a
sensible and competent run.

On 19 June I paid my last NCC visit to Cookstown. The
occasion was a return Sunday School excursion from Portrush
to Coalisland, the significant part of which appears in Table F.
Jimmy Simpson's handling of the tank engine was adequate
and if he had been taking *4* forward to Coalisland from
Cookstown I should certainly have gone too. However, *184*
with GNR crew was almost an everyday affair there and I
contented myself with listening to her raise the echoes as she
climbed towards Stewartstown. When I joined the train during
the running-round period at Cookstown Junction (prior to
1950 such excursions went, of course, via Kilrea) I found it
so extremely packed that I had to travel with the guard, that
lively character, Billy Black, one of Antrim's yard shunters
during the busy war years. It was a nostalgic chance that his
father had been a well known Cookstown guard in former
days. The local drivers on the 4.20pm ex Belfast in those days
had their work cut out keeping time with the small engines. . .
'You can't take any chances with Black. He'll put down every
minute.' Later the son received deserved promotion to platform inspector at York Road, where his energy was probably
not sufficiently appreciated till after he had retired.

Table K shows the last part of an enterprising run with the
Sunday 6.15pm ex Derry. Usually very well patronised, an
unusual feature for Derry–Belfast trains was nonstop running
between Coleraine and Ballymena, although the 39min
allowance was not unduly adventurous. Through the years,

travelling ticket collectors have caused less irritation on the
NCC than any railway I know but this was one train which
was invariably checked, usually by the guard, who actually
retained the tickets as he covered the train during that 39
minute session. Thus anyone joining at Ballymena would have
his ticket also retained at the barrier there, unusual practice
except for football excursions, where the idea would appear
to be that the gates at Belfast can then be opened wide on
arrival to disperse any possible hooligans as quickly as
possible.

98 had come from the 'shops and a typical job in such
circumstances was for her to haul *66* up from Coleraine on
25 June. At Ballymoney a large number of scrap cattle wagons
were attached and later, at Cookstown Junction, *62* and *69*
also. Shortly afterwards the scrap merchants dealt with this
derelict contingent, as well as sister engines *58* and *64*. *57* had
returned after two years on the Great Northern and on 17
June *7* piloted *99* on the 3.45pm ex Belfast as far as Antrim.
Here an Adelaide driver, Joe Graham, took her over and thus
another transfer was effected.

Another tank engine provided a diversion on Sunday, 11
July when signalman Allen at Coleraine insisted that Derry
driver Ned Curran examine *3* before proceeding with the
Derry portion of the 11.25am ex Belfast. He based his reluc-
tance to give the train a clear road on some marks on the
crossing beside his cabin. Sure enough it soon transpired that
the engine had a broken spring. This signalman's brother at
Castlerock was another sharp individual. During that period
he would observe me about his station from time to time and
then, some fifteen years later, I chanced to be driving past
Bellarena station when the same man, perched on the top of a
large tractor, hailed me with, 'That's a nice way for a railway
enthusiast to be travelling about.'

4 passed through Magherafelt again on 12 July with an
Orangemen's special from Kilrea, but the NCC big guns were,
as usual, being concentrated on an operation which invariably
affected them even more, the Apprentice Boys' celebrations

in Derry in August. So great was the traffic that the 3pm ex Belfast was terminated at Eglinton with 'bus connection into Derry, thus leaving a clear road for a succession of return specials. Those to Belfast were worked by *95, 96, 97, 98* and *100*, the Coleraine ones having *102* and *104*. *95* had been the Ballymena engine most of the summer and very apt it would have been, with her name, to see her on that town's special to Derry but it was *94* which hauled it.

Tables E, G, H, K, L and M each include one example of 1954 running. After Cole's run with *94* he described her as 'a good wee engine' and indeed this effort by her on a stopping train was more lively than several others the same week with his regular engine of that period, *98*. Another driver who wasn't afraid to raise the echoes, Bobbie Miller, continued on past Castlerock with *76* (Table M), the run being almost indistinguishable from another a few days previously with the same driver and *75*. As regards the up runs, that of *92* is just another glimpse of pre-war quality from this lovely engine. As far as the 5.30pm was concerned, McClements would not have been my choice for a fast run, but considering the consistently heavy loads this week, he did well, the one included being the best amongst the three engines he had, *99, 101* and *103*.

The onset of the winter timetable produced action, as usual, to store engines at Whitehead. *13* hauled *57* thence on 2 September and a week later *15* dealt with *100*, both stored engines being outshopped as recently as July. *81* and *74* came forth from the works about the same time and these were the last 4-4-0s to be repaired for over a year. Those who have resented the Anglification of the NCC might have observed that by now almost all this class were running with the standard LMS tender. Withdrawn engines *77, 79, 82* and *83* had passed their tenders to *73, 84, 86* and *72* during the year, leaving *85, 87* and the three V1 class 0-6-0s with the only signs of BNCR inheritance.

Five engines were now being regularly treated with Botan. For *8* at Larne and *54* and *97* at Belfast the dosage was 10lb, while *91* and *101* at Coleraine were to have 8lb. Despite this

J

there was very little sign of any hanging back by *101* but *91* resisted such modern ideas with frequent bouts of severe priming. At Belfast Keenan and Wilson now had *97*. The former driver used to call me over, fix me with that heavy gaze and then recount a complicated tale about that 'oul Botan', but I imagine he really enjoyed a problem, so great was his interest in the steam locomotive, sustained right until his death, aged seventy-five, in October 1971.

On 5 November *14* penetrated the remains of the Drapers-town branch, closed over four years previously. The main purpose of this exercise was the loading of telephone poles, for which a train of six timber trucks and van had been supplied. Inspector W. Hanley was in charge, well prepared for trouble with bins of sand, both wet and dry, all very necessary as the track was very overgrown. An unexpected obstacle was McColgan's crossing where Derry County Council had resurfaced and rolled a road over the permanent way, but inspector and crew cut a track through with hammer and chisels. The journey from Magherafelt took three hours and the return trip, during which the loading was done, half as long again. Driver Magill and fireman T.H. Ramsey made the water last out ten hours until the tank could be refilled at Magherafelt. Five days later another trip completed the job after successfully navigating the menace of Desertmartin siding, where the facing points were by now in a very dangerous state.

On the Great Northern an excuse frequently resorted to by enginemen for failure to recover lost time has, especially in the postwar era, been that any unusually high speed would produce adverse reactions from the dining-car staff. This unreal world of rather fragile looking waiters intimidating robust enginemen had no parallel on the NCC, so one can imagine a tongue in cheek investigation: on 1 November driver H. Wallace of Derry had been the cause of consider-able breakage of crockery (and stout and whiskey bottles) whilst in charge of the 3.15pm ex Derry. This happened approaching Coleraine and no doubt Wallace, in his defence, emphasised his anxiety to have the speed reduced from 60mph to the regulation 25mph on the Bann bridge. The sudden braking here is traditional, a last minute curtailment to an exciting sprint from Castlerock.

A year previously, important action had begun as regards boilers for the smaller engines, and now the position, in this respect, of at least five of the moguls had to be considered, as it was ten years since *90-93* and *96* had had anything done. *90* had now *96*'s boiler of 1935 and it was decided to withdraw the doyen mogul, including the boiler, though she was not sold, finally, till two years later. *93*, with *91* not so far behind, had the most mileage done so it was decided to reboiler these two engines, leaving *92* and *96* (both better running engines, to my mind) to struggle on for a few more seasons, as far as traffic demanded. A boiler off *99* had been ready for some time with a new firebox and this was fitted to *93*, after *91* had been given *104*'s reconditioned boiler. During the next seven years only one mogul, *100*, had her boiler changed. Of all the moguls only one ran with the same boiler throughout her entire life, *103*. This was a very rare situation though seven of the 2-6-4 tanks, of course, were scrapped still retaining their original boiler. The only other cases of this which occur to me in the period after World War I were five 4-4-0s built using some old parts, so possibly unlikely to outlive a boiler. These were *3, Glenaan, 28, County Tyrone, 60, County Donegal, 61, County Antrim* and *33, Binevenagh.*

The excellent NCC system of keeping most of the crews on the same engines began to be less rigorously applied from about this time, especially as regards the York Road tank link, from which McCune had just retired. On 29 September *72* had been replaced on the GNR by *4* (possibly for standardisation purposes) and sometimes this engine or *74* would provide a welcome change to the inevitable 2-6-4 tank on Larne line trains.

CHAPTER 6

Wind of Change:1955-7

Now that the Bangor line had been completely dieselised for a year, plans could be implemented towards similar 'modernisation' of the NCC. Because of the management's infatuation with the multiple unit system it was natural that they should commence with the more local type of train, so mainline workings remained, for the most part, steam during the period covered by this chapter.

1955

This New Year came in with the engines giving more trouble, particularly as regards steaming, than I could ever remember. Sometimes this was due to fine coal but most complaints were directed at the use of Botan instead of the old system of regular washing out of boilers. There was little trouble on the Larne line where the loads were light for the gradients, but even there it was noticeable that when *8*'s fortnight for working the heavy 5.50pm boat train came round her time-keeping was uncertain. With *54* too, at Belfast, there were several cases of much loss of time with the 5.10pm to Ballymoney. The moguls too were frequently shy of steam, especially *91*.

An interesting case was *104*, which on 5 January arrived at Ballymoney with the 5.30pm ex Derry with both injectors on.

Yet so rapidly was the water being consumed that Quinn had only half a glass of water to start the climb to Dunloy, though the engine steamed well enough to permit the exhaust injector to be on the whole way to Ballymena. However, at the summit the left injector had to be used as well and the overall picture was one of terrific consumption of both coal and water, if time was to be maintained. This engine was only a few weeks out the the 'shops and remembering how long it had taken to get her working right after the previous overhaul her performance was now studied carefully, even to the extent of the inspector going out to Coleraine on the 10pm and returning with the 3am goods. The next day, 12 January, Chambers of Derry (temporarily driving from Coleraine shed), an unruffled character if ever there was one, gave a good report on *104* after a trip up on the 11.5am ex Derry. Two days later on the same train Nemesis punished such confidence with a mishap which might have been a disaster if it had happened a couple of minutes later. Near Mossley a tender tyre came off *101* but fortunately the engine stayed on the road and was hauled slowly to Greenisland along the 'back line' a few hours later.

However, by 21 January *101* was once again displaying her strong untemperamental personality by arriving 2min early at Belfast with the heavy 3.15pm ex Derry (ten bogies ex Coleraine). Prior to working the 2.20pm Coleraine–Portrush she had had a full dose of Botan and without taking water at Portrush, or coming up, had still 1400 gallons left in her tender on this winter day.

While *101* carried all before her, the other Coleraine engine with Botan, *91*, was in dire distress on 29 January with the 8.25am. Davie Brangam had been expecting trouble, for there had been a very bad knock from the big end coming up with the 3am goods. At the platform a fitter was summoned but before he arrived they got the right away. However, he had to stop the 8.25 at Greencastle and it was nearly half an hour before *96* came up behind the train, pushing it all the way up to Ballyclare Junction, where it was discovered that *91* had a badly cracked cylinder. Some weeks later, near Bellarena, with the 10.25am, Dan O'Kane apparently omitted to put on *94*'s blower before shutting off for a slack and she blew back, badly burning the inspector's coat.

The 10pm Belfast–Coleraine was one train I never had occasion to use and soon after this time it was, of course, cut back to Ballymena with bus connection forward. On 27 April passengers on it had the experience (particularly infuriating at such a late hour) of arriving 57min late, after *91* had had to be hauled from Ballymoney. Thereby hangs a tale though this may not have been the precise occasion of its denouement.

About this time curtailments in services in the Derry area had resulted in some redundancy at Derry shed. This happened to coincide with retirements and some sickness at Coleraine so Bob Chambers and Paddy O'Kane were given suitable jobs in the links at Coleraine, which they could work but still continue to live in Derry. One turn involved taking over the 8.25am ex Belfast at Coleraine, working the 11.35am ex Portrush and then back to Coleraine with the 3.45pm ex Belfast. O'Kane had to travel out of Derry on the 7.5am to be on the platform ready to take over the 8.25 engine so that by the time they ran into Portrush he would be ready for the usual cup of tea. Brangam and his fireman, as they handed over at Coleraine, had assured O'Kane that the fire had been cleaned at Belfast (the normal practice) but it was soon discovered that this was very far from the truth. So by the time it had been done at Portrush there was no time for tea and O'Kane was furious. The same thing happened again the next day and the driver was quite prepared to report the whole matter, only to be restrained by the fireman, who knew a trick worth two of that.

So the pair bided their time all through the following week until it was the job of the guilty crew to be taking over the 3.45pm which O'Kane was still working. The usual practice at Belfast for Coleraine moguls was to clean the fire at the ash dump and then wait near the foreman's office until it was time to back onto the train. On this famous occasion, however, *91* did not appear from the ash dump till the last minute for not only had they not cleaned the fire but they had been filling a convenient part of the tender with a good supply of clinker to shovel into the firebox at the last minute before handing over to Brangam. This was done and their successors did nothing at Portrush, for on this turn they themselves would be handing over at Ballymoney to a Belfast crew and taking their engine for the 9pm goods ex Ballymoney as far as Ballymena. Yet another Belfast crew worked *91* out of Belfast on the 10pm and the psychology of O'Kane's mate was faultless; no one yet had cleaned that fire. At Ballymena Brangam got *91* back again and you have already been told the kind of trip he had.

While footplate gamesmanship of this subtle order was being practised the authorities were having the German MAK diesel tested. Hanley tried her all over the system on both passenger and goods so that on 19 April she was hauling the Kilrea goods. General opinion seemed to be that this was a good machine, even if it had come from the GNR and (originally) Germany. Steam enthusiasts may well be grateful for the laissez-faire kind of muddle which prevented this type being extended beyond the one example, which soon returned to the GNR. It wasn't fast enough, of course, for mainline passenger services, but no doubt the makers could soon have remedied that.

On 15 June I enjoyed a sprint up from Ballymena in 34min 53sec on the 5.30pm ex Derry with *98* and 270 tons, but driver Adamson was far from pleased with her, complaining that the driving wheels had been slipping badly at speed. One mogul seemingly immune from mechanical complaint, no matter how badly the others behaved, was *99*. From the previous summer and right through the winter she had, as usual, been working from Coleraine shed, mainly on the 5.25 pm ex Belfast. Her mileage of 54,607 in 1954 had only twice been exceeded since 1950; by herself in 1952 and by *104* in 1953. At last she went to the 'shops and upon reappearing during the last week in April went back to Coleraine, though now on the 3.15pm job. Within a few weeks she was back in

Belfast with her buffer beam split from top to bottom. This had apparently been caused by some horseplay at the shed on the part of Coleraine's young cleaners. Even the most light-hearted NCC engineman shook his head a little at this. It was not respectful treatment for *99*.

3 June seems a suitable point to refer to the MED units for the first time, now wholly responsible for Bangor line operation. That evening a six-car set reached York Road from Queens Quay and the following morning the 7.35am to Whitehead and 8.15am to Larne was each three-car set. The AEC unit 6/7 was also now working from Larne. All this in a minor key was in logical counterpoint to the moguls as they slipped almost imperceptibly from grace, though a few had nearly ten years of life left.

Interesting delay was caused at Coleraine on 25 June when *97* worked eleven empty carriages from Portrush, off a GNR excursion, into Henry's siding and then could not clear the points. The following Friday the BBC broadcast from the footplate of *100* on the journey of the 5.25pm between Castlerock and Derry.

12 July produced some workings of considerable territorial interest. *6* worked empty carriages from Greenisland to Kilrea for an Orangemen's special and *10* was to follow 35 minutes later but first had to bring assistance to Monkstown where the points had jammed. Her train was for Maghera and another in the evening was worked to Randalstown by *54*. The ordinary 9.25am had had twelve bogies, *50* piloting *98* as far as Dunloy, from which she had to return to Belfast at speed as the loco inspector, aboard, was required urgently there for a diesel emergency.

98, after two recent derailments at Portrush turntable, was again derailed on 25 July. This time it was at the ash disposal dump at Belfast, a conveniently harmless place though it took most of the day to get her on the road again. Three days later came a near disaster and another black mark against the moguls. *92* was piloting another mogul on the 11.25am ex Belfast when the right hand coupling rod broke about half way causing considerable damage to the framing, cab and other fittings. Trains normally are moving at their fastest at this point, just beyond Dunadry, so it was very fortunate that both engines stayed on the rails. Fortunate too, was the decision of 92's fireman, Percy Mitchell, to brush the footplate near the feet of his driver, Bob McKeown, as otherwise he must have been struck by the flailing rod. Today that brush occupies a place of honour in Mitchell's home. The crew of the train engine was John McAllister and Willie Cameron.

Table H shows two good runs by McAllister from the same period which suggest little nervous reaction, though certainly in 99's case he did show more restraint on the viaduct than usual. The run out of Derry with this train appears in Table N and I recollect comments by the crew about the rough riding of 104, with the slack cab constantly striking the whistle during running. The prelude to 91's effort might have pleased the photographer, for the 5pm ex Portrush had two carriages headed by two engines, nose to nose, Stewart Wilmot driving 103 and John Keenan 75.

This summer the main Ballymena job was slightly altered. The engine which came up with the 7.17am ex Cullybackey now left Belfast with the 10.25am as far as Coleraine, returning with a 1.50pm stopping train to Ballymena. An unusual engine to be shedded at Ballymena, 57, was on this job most of the summer, also working the 3.50pm Ballymena-Belfast. The Derry-Larne Harbour through train of previous summers ran now only on Saturdays though there were still, of course, the through coaches off the 3.15pm at 5.37pm from Ballyclare Junction. It was strange now on Saturdays to observe Ballymena men on the famous 8.25am and on 6 August there was another rupture with the dining car staff when 3 was backing onto the Derry portion of this train at Coleraine. Dan O'Kane came against the train unduly hard. He seems to have been in a hurry that day as the guard was left behind at Downhill, much to the amusement of the usual onlookers in holiday spirit at that superbly sited halt.

September brought a typical effort by T.J. McAuley (Table

L), the only pity being that *94* did not have more time to recover. A few days later a BCDR crew of Girvan and Bennett stabled *94* in Whitehead for the winter. Of the surviving 'Derby' moguls *93* was in charge of drivers Wilson and Keenan at York P ad. Her appearance was now certainly not improv d by the Stanier chimney given her when the boiler had been changed, but her good behaviour continued to be reliable. *92* was out again after her mishap, as free-running and economical as ever, but there was now a severe vibration at the trailing end plus a slight tendency to slip at speed. Tests showed eventually that the engine was badly out of line. Coleraine was having to persist with *91* and she still appeared very frequently on the 8.25am. On 30 August with McClements on an 8.25am of ten bogies she dropped 11 minutes to Kingsbog summit, slipping incessantly from Bleach Green to beyond Mossley. However, a boiler inspection of this engine showed that Botan was keeping the tubes in fine condition.

On 8 September *13* and *14* were off for repairs and *15* was allowed to go on the Kilrea goods, leaving no suitable engine for the Carrickfergus shunting job. After some discussion, the 0-6-0 tank *19* was sent. When tested en route at Greenisland for signs of heating none were found, but the tank was not risked for the 2.45pm passenger ex Carrickfergus, another engine being sent from Belfast. *18* was also in daily use at that period but a year later failed to convince authority that another overhaul would be justified.

One of the high-sided tenders lost a tyre for the second time this year on 30 September when *103* was derailed on the crossover as she was leaving Antrim with the 6.35pm. *86* went down next morning with the breakdown van and it was decided that for hauling up to Belfast the mogul would have to be turned. This operation took most of the day, *103* having the unusual experience of Antrim turntable (minus tender) after which the tender was coupled up again. Unusually for the NCC a kind of panic seemed for a time to follow this, complaints being made about the riding of moguls *91, 93, 101* and *102*. Another kind of complaint came from Portrush where a 'gentleman' and his wife, strolling along Golf Terrace, were deluged by smuts from the chimney of *3*, in No 1 platform.

So I spent a day on the mainline to see for myself, some of the results of which appear in Tables C and L. To my mind things seemed to be going as well as ever and *99*'s work on the 10.25am had been quite brilliant. Yet I was no sooner back in Belfast than news came through that that very engine was now, in fact, lying beyond Monkstown, on the 5.25pm, with a burst tube. Word about this was smartly passed through before the departure of the 5.43pm stopping train and eventually this train was combined with the 6pm to Dunloy, *50* piloting *95*.

The winter timetable revealed just about the leanest mainline operations since the 1933 strike. Out of Derry the last departure of the day was the 5.30pm express, the goods now leaving at 11.20am and reaching Coleraine at 3.45pm after 1¾ hours wait at Limavady Junction. That branch was now completely closed, as was the Cookstown one, from Magherafelt. So Derry's two tanks (*3* and *55*) between them worked the 7.5am, 8.30am, 11.20am goods, and 3.15pm ex Derry, returning from Coleraine with the forward portions of the 8.25am, 10.25am, 3.45pm and 5.25pm ex Belfast. The 11.5am ex Derry was worked by the mogul which had arrived with the 5.40am goods ex Coleraine, the 1.10pm by the 4-4-0 off the 8.15am ex Coleraine and finally the 5.30pm by the Coleraine engine which had worked the 11.25am into Derry. Ballymena too had come down badly in status. Apart from shunting the yard at Ballymena Goods, the workings were down to four as follows: 6.48am passenger ex Cullybackey, 11.35am goods to Randalstown and Antrim, 3.20pm goods to Greenisland, and 5.30pm passenger, Cullybackey to Belfast. The return workings of these were: 9.25am passenger ex Belfast, 5.30pm Aldergrove to Ballymena, 6pm Belfast-Dunloy with empty carriages back to Cullybackey, and 10pm ex Belfast. For these jobs the usual engines were *50, 84, 81* and *74*.

On paper, at any rate, economies were going to be considerable for most Larne line workings were now MED units, though Larne still had four tanks for the peak period trains. The diesel operations, especially on Sundays, were beset with failures with irritating delays to the public, something the older men (who by seniority were usually first to be trained on the diesels) found hard to reconcile with the reliability to which they were accustomed.

Of more interest was the behaviour of *98*, the problem child of the moguls, now that *97*, after a period in disgrace on Ballymena locals, had gone to the 'shops for a further attempt to revitalise her into the excellent machine she had once been. Adamson's experience with *98* now came to mind when there were more complaints, from both Coleraine and Belfast drivers, about frequent slipping at speed,even when shut off. So the 'shops had a look at her for a few weeks but whatever they did to *98*, Adamson had her back on 15 December when working the 3.45pm ex Belfast and he sent an urgent message back to Belfast that *98* was now worse than ever. Inspector Hanley therefore went out to make the journey back with her on the 5.30pm ex Derry. The result was, however, that the behaviour of *King Edward VIII* was as stubborn as the monarch commemorated, for no matter what they did on the footplate, *98* would not slip.

At about the same time York Road police barracks had some success when they were able to return various footplate fittings stolen from two withdrawn BCDR locomotives, *216* and *229*, which goes to show that the 1968-70 activities, whereby mogul tanks were frequently raided in search of copper, were not unique on the NCC. Fortunately engines in store that winter, such as *57* and *92* in Cookstown Junction, were not molested.

Thus Christmas approached and with it possibly some Christmas spirit, for it seems that the driver and fireman of *93* on Coleraine ballast duty on a December Sunday were

Page 141   GOODS TRAFFIC AT ANTRIM, WITH 4-4-0s, CLASS U2
(above) 86 with 6.25pm (Saturdays only) ex Belfast, 19 June
1954; *(below) 84* arriving with 7.40am Kilrea-Belfast,
September, 1956. *74* is shunting, prior to working Aldergrove
train.

Page 142 (above) 3.15pm goods ex Belfast approaching Monkstown Junction with *5* assisted in rear by another 2-6-4 tank, *1*, 15 October 1960; *(below)* Class V1 0-6-0 *13* shunting at Castledawson, 21 September 1956

suspected of dropping a generous supply of coal to every crossing keeper and ganger between Calf Lane and Downhill. The humanity of the NCC is once again evident in that, although much energy was expended in getting proof of what exactly transpired, no actual punishment was ever applied, as far as I have been able to ascertain.

At the same time precious little benevolence was being shown by the authorities towards the various engines whose boiler position was now becoming serious, money instead being expended on re-engining (already) the entire fleet of twenty-eight MED units. No doubt the diesel advocates could point at eighteen quite new tank engines as adequate resources if diesels proved inadequate for heavy traffic.

However, *80*, which was to run the greatest 4-4-0 mileage every year from 1956 forward, was overhauled in November with the boiler out of *72*. The workshops then turned their attention to *100*, whose firebox was life-expired. *102*'s frames did not justify any more patching and this engine as a whole had been suspect for some time, so *100* got her boiler, and *102*, which had taken such a terrible pounding when new, became the second mogul to be withdrawn.

1956

The New Year seemed mainly concerned with the final arrangements for a massive sale of withdrawn locomotives. NCC ones were in the minority to BCDR engines, but Messrs Cohen & Sons Ltd, scrap merchants, were now the owners of *70, 79, 82* and *83*, lying at Carrickfergus, and *71* and *77*, brought up from Ballymena.

The day of the grand auction, 19 January, seemed a significant one to test ex-BCDR diesel loco 28 on Monkstown bank. A sensible precaution was first taken of letting the mainline train (11.25am) away first. 28 then moved off with seven coaches but came to a halt on the first rise after Greencastle. *13* was about to leave for the Carrickfergus shunting duty so this engine pushed 28 and her train through to Monkstown, to clear the way for the 12.5pm to Larne Harbour. Nothing as onerous was ever attempted with 28 again and indeed there seems just a faint aroma of contempt about the approach to the result of this test. In fairness it should be stated that 28 had given several years of splendid service on light NCC trains immediately after the closure of the BCDR main line. How welcome it was, for instance, on Whitehead locals compared to the uncomfortable and foul-smelling railcars 1-4.

On 5 January *15* had been a surprising and not very welcome loan to Adelaide shed, possibly to compensate for having recalled all other NCC engines from the GNR. By May, however, she was back on the NCC, and the following year (1957) is the only one between 1952 and 1966 when a NCC engine was not based on the Great Northern. 26 February produced yet another revised timetable, mainly concerned with the reinstatement of goods trains abandoned, not very realistically, the previous October. So there was once again an evening goods out of Derry (7.45pm).

Of various mishaps during the next few months possibly the most interesting was the result of the collapse of *94*'s left piston head at Ballymena on 5 May. Driver Ritchie not only continued to Coleraine on this 5.55am with Ballymena shunting engine *86* but kept her for the return trip through to Belfast. Considering the restoration to life in modern times of Dhu Varren it is interesting to record a derailment at this sand siding on 8 June. *52* was the engine involved, having worked into Portrush with the 10.25am ex Belfast. On this turn 1½ hours at Portrush provided the opportunity for serving the siding. Operated from the tablet, the practice was to propel wagons from Portrush, the brake van leading.

The run with *6* in Table M is a reminder of an occasion, when, in order to photograph trains passing closed stations, I walked the track from Limavady Junction to Lisahally. On a pleasant midsummer day this is an even better way of 'learning the road' than on the footplate and since that time I have gradually 'walked' the entire NCC main line. A month later *85* provided typically spirited entertainment, as shown in

Table D. Retaining the Fowler type chimney till the end of her days this engine's crisp bark was recognisable from those with the more modern type. *76* was one of the first to receive the Stanier type and it was said she never steamed as well after that alteration.

The January sale must have been a great success for the accountants, for by the end of June an all out effort was being made to provide Messrs Cohen with further supplies. One had the feeling that if a very careful watch wasn't kept on any engine going out on a train it might be sold before it got to its destination. However, some of the victims were fairly obvious, such as BCDR engines *222* and *229* and the framing of another, *216*. Also *73* from Ballymena and *75* from Coleraine, in bad repair, could scarcely survive in such circumstances. On 23 June *18* was on her usual shunting duty but a week later she was sold. *101* had been suddenly taken out of service in March after doing the 8.25am turn consistently since her last repair in September last. The firebox in the boiler she had got off *95* in 1947 had at least 100,000 miles of life left but the boiler, itself, was now over the regulation twenty years of the NCC. One story had it that the tubeplate had gone. Another was that her scrapping was a blunder, a mistake on someone's part. Certain it is that in August they were breaking up *75* and *101* side by side in the morgue siding. Here during shunting Inspector Gourley stepped between the tenders of *90* and *97* (which now had *102*'s tender), forgetting that the buffers were off and was badly crushed and taken to hospital. Altogether, for all the old hands it was a sorry affair.

This summer's arrangement for the 3.15pm ex Derry was that on Saturdays during July and August the whole train went through to Larne Harbour, giving no service to Belfast. Also during those months there was a Wednesdays-only 8.30pm from Portrush which managed to reach Belfast in 90 minutes with stops at Portstewart and Ballymena. This was sluggish compared with 1938 but faster than contemporary facilities from Warrenpoint, which had less single line. On

145

Saturdays there was a schedule of over 2 hours (by one minute) to Portrush. This was the 11.30am, which got landed with a 4min crossing stop at Cullybackey and a 5min one at Dunloy, there being no Ballyboyland loop at that period. This train had to cope with the vans and passengers off the Larne boat train and on 7 July McClements had *98* for a load of eleven coaches and a van, *7* piloting to Kingsbog. This was the day that railcar 3 was burnt to a shell at Whitehead.

Since overhaul in December *97* had been spending môst of her time at Coleraine, still the subject of criticism for slack tyres, rough riding, periodical priming and a cracked framing. The 12 August celebrations in Derry generally indicate the current standing of the best engines and *100* and *103*, though also at Coleraine, were borrowed for the specials from Belfast. Another Belfast special had W.R. Wilson with *94* while *95* worked from Coleraine. These last two, suffering from leaking tubes, had been specially stopped the previous day for attention but *94* still gave some trouble on the way down so was exchanged for *99* for a return Belfast special, a Ballymoney special being more suited to *94* in this condition.

On 8 September, a few days after heavy overhaul, *55* smashed Dunloy gates with the 1.5am goods ex Belfast, BCDR driver J. Letman. A few days previously *94* had been about to leave with the 1.15pm to Portrush when the inspector noticed that the vacuum bag on the van behind the tender had collapsed. The guard, that splendid character, Tom Simpson, produced a spare one from his van and all hands turned to driver Sam Sloane for his bag of tools. However, the hammer had no head on it. Even more embarrassing was another incident at about the same time. Besides the problem of getting the diesels to run properly there was now trouble with heating and also the danger of fire. So various chiefs were given a run in one of the units to demonstrate new fire extinguishers at work. After a fire had been started deliberately not one of the new installations could be persuaded to work so it was fortunate some of the old variety were to hand.

On 22 September, just a few weeks after *101* had been

finally cut up, the Heysham boat arrived at Donegall Quay with the body of one of her most regular drivers, Jimmy McClements, who had died while on holiday in England. It was typical of the NCC that a wide spectrum of railwaymen should visit Coleraine for the funeral; from the operating superintendent, W.S. Marshall, past and present locomotive inspectors Bacon and Hanley, to a shed foreman from York Road, Joe Agnew, and drivers Cole, also from that shed, and Meneilly from Larne.

The frequency of mishaps at Portrush turntable is best emphasised by an alteration in the workings whereby the Derry tank replaced the 3.45pm mogul between Coleraine and Portrush. Moguls with the original smaller tender had less trouble on the turntables, but the policy was now to replace these with any large ones left over, due to withdrawals. So *91* was now running with *101*'s tender, and *103*, now stored in Carrickfergus, had given up her tender to *95*, about to emerge from the 'shops. *98* had been in trouble again on Sunday, 21 October when working the 10am ex Derry, this train being unusual for a Derry driver in that he worked south of Coleraine, to Ballymoney, where footplates were exchanged with Belfast men. On this occasion John Keenan had to give up *98* at Coleraine with a broken pony spring. Upon examination several faults were also found with *98*'s tender so the only solution was to give her the small one off *95*.

Ballymoney was in a different category from the other mainline stations of the NCC in that, without a running shed or a branch line, an engine was not often readily available for shunting the goods yard. As a result this station made regular use of a horse for shunting. Even more willing, however, was Ballymoney's human shunter, Jimmy Crawford, surely the most strictly honest in an occupation where straight dealing is traditional. On one occasion Crawford found a half-crown on the platform, handing it immediately to Stationmaster Mackarell, who gave it back to the shunter to keep if no one claimed it. In desperation Crawford then got rid of it through the slot in the gentlemen's lavatory. It was typical of his well-doing attitude that he had three daughters in the teaching profession, and his anxiety to be always busily employed ('bedad') in the yard was well known. Frequently when the engine from Coleraine had finished shunting and was ready to work back the goods, Crawford would be requisitioned as guard, rather than bring one specially from Coleraine. Memorable indeed was the afternoon when the Ballymoney signalman got the bell from Macfin unexpectedly and lifted the phone to ask what this train was he was accepting. From that outpost came the reply 'No train! It's just Jimmy Crawford passing into the section.' Indeed Crawford, upon arriving at Coleraine with the goods, had walked the 8 miles back to Ballymoney along the track in case he was required for any purpose before the time of the next train back.

On 21 November *74* worked fifteen wagons of coal to Muckamore, having a very tough time up through Mossley with the sanding out of action. She continued with the van to Ballymena and worked from there thirty-five loaded wagons of cement to Coleraine. Here the crew took over *87* and worked her back light to Belfast, leaving *74* and *76* now as the Coleraine 4-4-0s, with *78* stabled in Derry. Thus *Queen Alexandra* went up to the scrapyard under her own steam. Her mileage as class U2 was, not surprisingly, the lowest of them all, 589,090.

The most regular engine for the Kilrea goods was now *84* and this locomotive witnessed another last run on 24 November when driver William White retired from Magherafelt. Henceforward Belfast crews handled this train in its entirety.

1957

The year 1971 does not appear to have been affected by the 'seven year' theory, which evidences 1950, 1957 and 1964 as disastrous years for railways in the north of Ireland. On the NCC in 1957 it was more an uneasy feeling, rather than momentous happenings, and indeed more attention was naturally being focused on GNR closures and the rapid run-down of steam on CIE.

On 30 January *13* made an early morning trip to Randalstown to work some 'out of use' wagons to Cookstown Junction. Just before returning she got derailed and *1* was despatched to Randalstown with the breakdown van. By 1pm *13* was on the road again but her tender was still derailed and the Kilrea goods would soon be due in that long section. So *1* worked the wagons to Cookstown Junction and then took over the goods from *15* when it arrived there. The 0-6-0 then went back to Randalstown until *13*'s tender was rerailed, the two class V1 engines returning to Belfast together, with the breakdown train. *14* was now lying in Carrickfergus shed, withdrawn.

19 April found me in Magherafelt. Earlier in the day I had photographed *84* tender first as she passed through Knockloughrim with the 7.40am goods ex Kilrea and soon I made my way to Toome for a shot of the same train passing over the Lower Bann viaduct. For the railway photographer, however, these were difficult days. At the present time hooligans and terrorists can more or less act as they please in Ireland, but in 1957 there was much more strict control. A policeman soon approached my position near the bridge and decided to search me. This failing, apparently, to give much satisfaction, he seemed to be wondering what to do next when there was a shrill whistle and the official inspection car, carriage No 3, was propelled slowly over the bridge by *2*, in shining condition. This was quite unexpected as was W.S. Marshall's reaction, for he called down to me to join them for a trip to Kilrea. While I was sampling an excellent lunch in the carriage one constable was, no doubt, still occupied with his thankless task.

On 1 May Killagan signal cabin was burnt to the ground by terrorists, which soon resulted in the abolition of this rather useless block post. About the same time Dunloy cabin was also destroyed, an interesting example of lack of imagination on the part of the arsonists, for, twenty-six years before, these had been the two cabins selected for destruction. Also on the first day of May was the funeral of Sammy Mills of Coleraine who had been driving very recently and whose performances with *100*, especially, I can never forget. On that very day, indeed, *Queen Elizabeth* had twelve bogies on the 8.25am with *10* as pilot to Kingsbog. *100* had not been a frequent performer on this train in the past, but was now turning up very frequently.

Mills had been only one of several at Coleraine shed with a keen sense of humour and R.J. McCahon too had his own brand. The ballast engine, usually *74* at this period, was invariably in action on a Friday, and on this occasion had been summoned by P W Inspector Alec Malcolm to a job on the Portrush branch. As they passed slowly from the yard along past the up platform, fireman Frank Dunlop managed to collect their week's pay and jump back onto the footplate again. The driver's pay slip showed £9, quite a respectable figure for those days. The crew then decided to play a trick on the ballast guard, Sam Dinsmore, and they carefully altered the slip to £19. While work was being done on the track Dinsmore came along for the usual cup of tea and with great ingenuity the pair of knaves managed to let him see the pay slip. The poor man was so furious at the sad lot of guards compared to footplate men that he refused the tea and returned to his van.

Table N shows a run out of Derry with *98* on the 7.35pm. John Keenan was a good runner, though different in temperament from his brother Jimmy at York Road and from another brother Joe, porter at Antrim. *4*, with Ritichie driving, took this train over from Coleraine forward and an unusual event was the addition of *91* at Antrim as pilot. Apparently driver Palmer was in a hurry home, for with 270 tons the two engines scorched away to 64mph on the adverse section before Templepatrick, but a poor finish produced a time of 23min 21sec, when I thought we might possibly achieve even time.

In modern times the wise man keeps well clear of religious

and political demonstrations, but in 1957 it was quite possible to emerge unscathed from such proceedings. The run in Table B on 12 July was the prelude to a bus trip over to Kilrea that I might return with an Orangemen's special over the Derry Central. Unknown to me, however, *84* with Bob Logue and his fireman, Kerr, had stalled on the way down with one of the specials, thus upsetting the march schedule in the town. When I arrived *84* and *86* had just come in again from Magherafelt, where they had had to go for turning, and *13* was also there with Hanley in case more trouble was experienced. The area of Kilrea station seemed to be swarming with the notorious 'B' specials and I heard the loco inspector warn the enginemen to look out for them on the track. Getting away about 25min late *84* was banked out up the 1/139 by *13* for less than a mile, this engine then returning to pilot *86* with Palmer and McGarvey. My first ever rail journey had been made in a BCDR six-wheeler, which now provided sanctuary for my last Derry Central trip, for three were included in a train which also had a nice selection of nine bogies and a van, for the drums.

The last mainline steam summer passed into the winter timetable on 2 September, an interim one until the new MPD units could be put into service on express trains. For a month units 36 and 37 had been under test with drivers being trained, though many were only in the preliminary stages of learning to handle the older MED type. One test produced a nonstop run from Derry to Belfast in 101min but another was less satisfactory, the two units stalling at Monkstown with thirteen wagons of coal and a van. The train had then to be divided, a steam engine pushing the second part up to Ballyclare Junction.

At Belfast the main link was now composed of Adamson, Cole, McAuley, Tracey, Magill and Hannan, their turns being mainline goods at 1.5am, passenger at 5.55am, 8.25am, 12 noon and 3.40pm with a turn to Larne Harbour at 6.7pm. Another link at Belfast worked the 12.5am goods to Kilrea and 2.55am goods to Ballymena, as well as Larne line passenger at 8.15am and 4.55pm. Keenan now spent much of his time in the fireman's seat of a York Road shunting engine. On one occasion he dozed off while his young mate spent an unusually long time drinking tea in the shunter's hut and the fire was allowed to go out. Next morning he found that Inspector Hanley had humorously left a large bundle of sticks on his engine.

Coleraine drivers now brought steam into Belfast only twice each day, the 7.10am ex Portrush and the 12.40pm ex Derry. They still worked the 6.35pm ex Belfast but it was now a MED unit which they also had for the 4.35pm to Whitehead. It was on this turn that that fox-hunting guard, Parkhill, took a fancy to a boat at Whitehead and before the end of the week had actually bought it. The vessel was then placed, with the utmost difficulty, in the guard's compartment of one of the driving units. Well placed for the through run to Coleraine, the main problem now was some over-observant official at Belfast, so the driver kept a watchful eye on the train while Parkhill chatted up the main danger, Inspector Black. Having left York Road unobserved, Parkhill insisted that the driver make a stop at Macfin (closed but handy for his home) and fortunately the inspector on duty at Coleraine (and Weir and Pyper were both pretty alert men) did not question why they had taken so long to come from Ballymoney.

On 8 October 9 hauled ex BCDR *30* (for preservation) to Cookstown Junction where both engines were stabled. When 9 had arrived new at York Road in June 1947, Isaac Blackam had soon been one of the two drivers to whom she had been allocated and here he was, over ten years later, with a BCDR fireman, Clegg, assisting, in charge of her again after a spell of seven years when she had been shedded at Larne. 9's other driver of that early period, Charlie McGonagle, was to die the following March (1958) and Blackam himself on 31 May.

With footplate changing now almost as prevalent on the NCC as on British Railways (and the GNR) one might see a different mogul arrive at Belfast with the 3.15pm ex Derry every day of the week but *54* remained very constantly on the 10.55am during this period, going through to Derry and then back on the 3.15pm as far as Coleraine. On 6 December Allen and McConnell worked the 10.55am out of Belfast and *54* lost considerable time through lack of steam. Hanley happened to be in Coleraine investigating a derailment, so a competent report was soon available, that *54*'s brick arch was very bad and that a heavy fire did not appear to be half burned. While she took water, therefore, the firebars were rocked, long stroke, to reduce the fire's thickness and the response was so good that a 30min late departure from Coleraine was reduced by 7min during the run to Derry.

The derailment in question was one of the classic kind where an engine goes for a run by itself. Just before midnight the previous evening *104* had moved off down Henry's siding, striking a set of carriages so hard that the last one (compartment coach 181) had gone through the stopblock and incurred some damage. The mystery was never solved officially but there were, of course, many enginemen to confirm that the regulator had been very slack. One driver had even booked it so. While this investigation was going on and just before *54* struggled in, there was a phone call from Ballymoney to the effect that *97*, shunting the store road, was derailed. Knowing the NCC style of humour there seemed, just for a fleeting moment, a possibility that this might have been a legpull and certainly a moment later it was denied. Probably the engine was indeed off the road but rerailed almost immediately, the crew of course, preferring no investigation. Certainly there was some kind of wicked fairy about, for *91* had been in collision with a UTA stores lorry at Belfast· the previous week, again apparently with no one on the engine.

On 11 November no less than 16 minutes were dropped by Tracey and McAtamney between Coleraine and Ballymena on the 3.15pm ex Derry, so *80* was taken on as pilot. Investigation discovered that *6* had a ring missing from her blastpipe, and both top main steam pipes blowing. Already diesel maintenance was considered more important than steam and when six other tanks had their blastpipes examined by the inspector only one (7) did not have a missing ring.

From the official data, 5 had the greatest tank mileage for 1957, an engine seldom involved in failures or derailments, or, for that matter, in outstanding runs. Her total of 43,060 was exceeded by three moguls, *91, 100* and *95*, of which the latter was top, with 48,425 miles. *93* had run the most during 1956, 50,881 miles.

CHAPTER 7

The End of Steam?: 1958-61

Some readers may imagine that because it was still just possible to travel behind NCC 0-6-0s and 4-4-0s this was a better time on the NCC than ten years later when a 2-6-4 tank, in neglected condition, was the only steam possibility. Let me immediately disabuse (to use a favourite word of the UTA chairman of that period, George B. Howden) you of any such notion. They were grim days indeed and only bearable because NCC engines were performing so well on the Great Northern area.

No longer did a NCC driver, waste in hand, take a last look around his mogul engine in shining condition, while his fireman was busily employed on the footplate preparing for an efficient departure. The anonymity of the diesel was terrible and the vocabulary now used by those who had to discuss it seemed almost obscene. Terms like 'losing control', 'switching in', 'isolating', cutting out', 'fuse' and 'switch' were freely bandied about by various folk who had no understanding of a steam locomotive and would never have looked twice at one. These people had always seemed more interested in their own motor cars and the eruption of a diesel engine into noise was a much happier sound to most railway executives than sudden protest from safety valves. How one wished for the reappearance of Bowman Malcolm to chase them all into their little offices and let the steam men get on with the job of running the railway to time and serving the public at all times of the year and not just the slack ones.

1958

A dozen years after the one we are now about to discuss, a 'Lollipop' man could often be seen escorting Shore Road children, within shouting distance of Greencastle spoil sidings. I would only have had to mention one engine, *8*, to him and he would remember 11 January 1958 when he made the run shown in Table C. This was all they had at the shed that morning for Magill and a heavy train, an engine whose mileage would have warranted immediate entry to the works under normal standards of maintenance, which the steam engines by now were not getting. I had never timed a tank on the 8.25am before. Indeed, most Coleraine drivers of the 1946–55 decade would have held up their hands in horror at the suggestion. To be losing seconds only on each section was fine work even allowing for *84*'s help out of Ballymena.

As the month progressed the weather deteriorated and by 21 January there was considerable snowfall. That morning it took Hannan on *95* over 10 minutes to get the ten bogie 8.25am out of Ballymena after setting back many times. The cause was eventually determined as frozen brakes, Coleraine being reached 23min late. The new order might not have fared even as well so it was probably a fortunate decision which had arranged the commencement of the new diesel timetable as a little later, 2 February.

The NCC was the last Irish mainline to commence dieselisation and indeed by 1958 the passenger services on all other Irish mainlines were completely diesel except the GNR where, however, the expresses had been handed over to BUT units two years previously. However, it was typical of the NCC that once the break had been made their new schedules made every other Irish mainline look sluggish. I doubt if by this time the UTA management was as bus-minded as it had been. Certainly their progressive ideas about fast schedules produced an express service whose timings were more revolutionary and indeed more demanding than anything since on either the NCC or the GNR. The modest and somewhat cautious official comments from W.S. Marshall at the time compare strangely with a 1970 handout to the press by Hugh Waring, when a new Enterprise train was described as 'the most modern train in Europe'. There was something too from Mr Waring about this being the most important railway event for fifty years. Had he not heard, I wonder, about the Boyne or Bleach Green viaducts, or even about the North Atlantic Express?

It was unfortunate that timings like 110min Derry–Belfast lasted only until the summer timetable and that this seems to have been gradually increased ever since. However, during that first remarkable February steam did get a fling at those fastest ever schedules. By 12 February I had learned that *99* had replaced a MPD express and the following day I observed and photographed *54* arriving 1min early at York Road with the 2.50pm ex Derry. Even allowing for a rather trivial load of four bogies this sight was almost unbelievable, for even during the by now almost mythical days of the North Atlantic Express a general running standard of this kind had not been thought possible.

The first chance to do anything about it myself was Saturday but it was soon clear at York Road that the 8.30am would have MPD units. I had just time then to decide to go to Derry by GNR, with opportunity there to observe and take whatever chance might provide. I knew there would be steam as far as Portadown anyway, with the 8.20am Dublin train, and ten bogies at Great Victoria Street was a warming sight, even if *210* did not achieve 60mph anywhere with them. After that I managed another 30 miles of steam before Derry, *82* producing some NCC type running between Portadown and Dungannon and later *132*, tender first, trundled along the banks of the Foyle after Strabane in pleasant style. I shudder now to think what I might have missed if the 4-4-0 had been more than the 4 minutes late she was into Foyle Road. Derry may be of modest size (except in unemployment) for a city, but the walk between the two major stations was quite far enough if one had barely 13 minutes to cover the distance.

However, *2* was just backing onto the 2.20pm, five carriages, of which two had belonged to the North Atlantic set. John McAllister had been taking the last few seconds in an attempt to get some larger lumps of coal. Tables I and N show just what he persuaded out of this engine but I should add that this was actually done without taking water en route, impossible for most of the later members of this class, *2* being always regarded as exceptionally economical. Afterwards that conscientious guard Tom Simpson seemed even more pleased than McAllister, who simply said, 'With decent coal these engines could run this train to time any day.'

The following Monday everything was back to MPD haulage and if ever again running of this calibre was demanded officially from steam locomotives on the NCC I am not aware of it. The new diesels were soon working the Coleraine-Derry goods also so that the only steam departures now from Derry were 1.5pm and 3.15pm. Derry's local service was now non-existent, for not only had the 7am stopping train to Coleraine been abandoned but out of Derry, Culmore was no longer served, and Magilligan and Downhill had only one train, which called on request. The express timings between the two cities were a commendable idea, of course, and at that time the railway was part of the UTA, so the natural policy had to be buses for sparsely populated areas. In recent years something has been done to rectify this 'Inter-city' policy.

The 9.25am to Ballymena was still steam as was the 5.25pm, though the working timetable showed the latter as an MED set. On 17 March *78* had no less than six bogies for the 9.25am, the least patronised Ballymena train. It seemed clear that the UTA was now adopting the modern idea of running trains to suit diesel rosters and not the passengers. Tom Hagan was not the man to respond to an extra load and lost 3min to Ballymena on a 48min timing. However, 67mph through Dunadry was more than I expected from a 4-4-0 in 1958.

Page 159   GNR 4-4-0s on the NCC *(above)* S class *171* leaving Castlerock, 17 October 1970, with Railway Preservation Society
of Ireland special to Derry; *(below)* Qs class *135* passing
Killagan with Windsor Gospel Hall excursion returning from
Portrush to Adelaide (GNR), June 1959

Page 160 *(above) 104* approaching Coleraine with 2.40pm Belfast-Portrush, 18 August 1956. Railwaymen are using the roof of an ex-BCDR carriage to view a football match; *(below) 1* descending gradient between Mossley and Monkstown with 1.10pm Londonderry-Belfast, 13 March 1958

Having worked out of Ballymena again at noon this engine
spent the afternoon on local goods trips involving Randalstown and Muckamore and finished up, with a Ballymena
driver, on the 5.30pm ex Aldergrove, which followed that
strange working whereby a three car GNR diesel set was
propelled with the two old Ballymena bogies from Antrim.
84 continued to be the most regular engine on this turn, with
80 (Table H) working the 5.30pm Cullybackey-Belfast. *81*
had not lasted after the previous summer, and after *76* had
been hauled up from Coleraine late in 1957, *85* and *86* were
also regarded as redundant in the diesel age, leaving only five
4-4-0s on the NCC.

On 22 March *50* had a football special for the Irish cup and
lost 20min between Derry and Belfast. Two days later *56* had
to come off the 3.15pm at Coleraine after losing 30min
through shortage of steam, being replaced by *95*. Many of the
enginemen seemed to be falling in with the management's
attitude that steam was finished, and would make little effort.
How remarkably indeed the running of the 1966-8 period
compares with most steam activities during the period of this
chapter. If the quality of work was poor, there was still pleasure daily observing the arrival of the heaviest train of the day,
the 3.15pm which still, until the end of the summer timetable,
had a couple of carriages and van detached at Ballyclare Junction for working to Larne Harbour. During the March-May
period I observed *91, 93, 94, 97* and *99* on the 3.15pm at
different times. *103, 96* and *98* seemed unlikely to run again,
the emergence of the latter a couple of years later being
likened unto that of Lazarus.

Few railways are transformed as much by the holiday
season as the NCC and with the traditional excursions in June,
Portrush station started to look, on Saturdays at any rate, like
her old steam self. On 21 June there were two steam specials
as well as the ordinary 7.30pm and 8.25pm to Belfast, both
steam. Johnny Fitzpatrick had *91* for the 8.25pm but discovered around teatime, when the firemen are either asleep
or viewing the girls on the strand, that this engine had two

L.

broken pony springs. He therefore took *The Bush* as far as Coleraine on the 7.30pm, changing there to *55* which he worked light to Portrush for the 8.25pm. This engine had been intended for Dunlop to work a 7.22pm return excursion to Derry, so *78* was lit up for this. *50* worked a 7.10pm special back to Belfast.

A week later the yearly excursion was run from Carrickfergus to Portrush. *9* worked this, with a BCDR crew, travelling via the 'back line' whereas in modern times this excursion has had to go into Belfast. Table A shows a hurricane effort from *7* the same day. The sad contrast between her driver's mood that day and his death a few years later is extreme, for he was found alone and uncared for several days after he had died.

The famous *2* was in trouble on 26 July with the 7.30pm ex Portrush. Failure, due to a damaged cylinder, occurred near Macfin, possibly caused by excessive priming, but there was also evidence of lack of lubrication. The same day *95* had given me a run out of Belfast so excellent that I could not but deduce that it must be so much speeding with the MPD units which was causing young men like Jimmy Simpson to wonder what was the best steam could do in comparison. (Table C.)

Tables A and K show how well the late Albert McClelland had adapted himself to NCC engines and conditions. The run with *9* had produced my first 'eighty' on a Portrush train for five years. On 26 September this engine was transferred to the GNR and three days later she was joined at Adelaide by *51*. The following day the Great Northern Railway ceased to exist and the role of the NCC locomotive department changed from that of a fairly benevolent neighbour to that of actual responsibility. No one on the GNR had much doubt how it would work out and a quick comparison of the average age of GN locomotives with those available on the NCC was a convincing factor.

York Road still managed a brave display of moguls for the Apprentice Boys' day in Derry. They sent *94, 95* and *104* on specials at 7.10am, 7.25am and 8.40am. At Coleraine *54* and

8 were specially cleaned, the latter working the Ballymoney special. Ballymena men were also responsible for two specials, *97* working the Randalstown one. *93* was booked for the Ballymena special and it was only frantic last minute work on a large tube, reported at Derry a week before, which enabled her to be turned out. No effort was spared to make these big days at Derry a success. Even the 'steam guns' used for cleaning the tubes of the tank engines were sent up from Coleraine and Derry a few days previously for repair, and there would be a wagon of good coal in a siding at Derry. On this occasion, after all the specials had gone down, Mechanical Engineer Courtney himself went down to Derry in a diesel train to have a look at an operation rather beyond the capacity of most bus companies.

On 24 September *19* brought a railcar trailer (511) from York Road to Mazefields via the Queens Bridge tunnel, but an even more unusual visit to a foreign domain occurred on 1 November when *13* failed at Antrim with the Kilrea goods. 0-6-0 *175* had arrived with the GNR goods and it was decided that she could take over from *13*, a tank engine arriving later to work the morning passenger from Antrim GNR. This example of inter-usage was later extended by an arrangement whereby the morning goods from Grosvenor Road GNR worked through to Ballymena, the passenger train for Great Victoria Street starting from there at 7.3am. Not only did this now make it unnecessary for Ballymena to have to find an engine for a connecting train to Antrim, but a through train from Ballymena to Lisburn etc may well have suited some passengers. So GNR 0-6-0s became quite common in Ballymena at this early hour, though NCC tanks also frequently worked this turn, as soon as Adelaide had more than the two necessary to keep the Dundalk workings going.

Only six steam engines were repaired at York Road during 1958, the lowest in NCC history until the last year of steam repair, 1965, when four were done. No tender engines were involved in either year, but the years in between tell a surprisingly different story.

1959

It was around this time that a confident prophecy from the top end of the table was made to the effect that 'There'll not be a puff of steam about the place by 1960.' Steam morale was low enough at the time for some to accept this as a sound and sensible comment so it was quite a surprise, before this year had scarcely begun, to observe outside York Road works a 1933 mogul in glittering ex-shop condition. This was *91* and it was nearly two months before she went into service. At that time there were no others of this class being used.

On 13 March *91* hauled *100* over to Adelaide, for breaking up, and the following day worked the 12 noon to Dundalk, the first time a mogul had worked an ordinary GNR train since the exchange between *96* and *170* in 1935. A few days later *56* appeared from the 'shops but early examination revealed a lamentable number of defects for an overhauled engine.

103 was still stored at Carrickfergus with a small tender and on 20 March *53* hauled *93* to join her there, the usual space for hibernation at Whitehead being occupied by the weed-killer. With a good boiler one would have thought *The Foyle* a suitable subject for overhaul if more moguls were needed for GNR requirements but in fact it was *97* which was outshopped on 25 April, being quickly passed to them on 12 May after being thoroughly tested. She travelled via Greenisland, from which *76, 85* and *86* were hauled to join *100* in a sad line of withdrawn engines at Adelaide. A surprising visitor to Greenisland on 19 June was a GNR 4-4-0 *202* (by now renumbered *67*). After having a few jobs done at York Road she also reached Adelaide afterwards by this route, hauling *14* and collecting another withdrawn engine, *78*, at Antrim. This cavalcade had scarcely passed over the Sixmilewater bridge before *54* arrived at Antrim with the 11.35am goods ex Ballymena and got derailed in the goods yard.

As a contrast to all this the standard of performance I experienced was high. Table A shows the burly Leathem

flashing down past Dunadry in the eighties with *3* and a
month earlier on the same 1.10pm his run with *7* and a slightly heavier train had been almost as fast. On 13 June *6* had
this train and I was fortunate not to be on a run where Palmer
and McAtamney had a bad time with a faulty injector. The
following Saturday I was travelling and found *1* backing onto
the train in No 3 platform, with appalling black smoke pour-
ing from her chimney. Just then Billy Hanley passed up and
commented, 'I would say that that engine had been prepared
in a great hurry.' Indeed, it transpired that *1* had not even
been lit up till 11.50am and with time up the pressure was a
mere 130lb. It occurred to me that this was an interesting trio
indeed on the footplate: the inspector with a problem and a
challenge, driver Tracey, the best type of man to accept
advice, and fireman Mitchell, who had had far too many
rough years on the moguls to get upset about a slight shortage
of steam. Table E shows the latter part of this run.

This was the day when a dull run back with Heffron on the
8.25pm, nonstop (to the public) from Portrush in 95 minutes
was enlivened a little by an unexpected act of desperation by
a middle-aged man in the compartment containing both sexes
in which I had managed to find a seat at the window. After
shouting to the rest of us 'Look the other way!' he proceeded
to relieve himself through the window, an unanswerable case
against the NCC practice of sending compartment stock on
65 mile journeys.

By now *56* had also gone over to the GN section and on 25
July *53* replaced *9* there. The exchange appeared to be somewhat impromptu. *53* had spent that Saturday morning shunting at York Road, before John Scott took her over to work
empty carriages to Portrush for return traffic. Scott was due
out of Portrush again with the ordinary 7.30pm but progress
with *53* was so poor that after 7pm he was only at Portstewart.
9 was in Portrush with a GNR excursion so this engine was
placed, instead, on the 7.30pm, Scott changing over as soon as
he reached Portrush. Thus *53* reached the GNR in charge of
the excursion and it is possibly better that I have no record of

when *9* arrived at York Road, as her tablet catcher had been removed on transfer to the Great Northern.

Table B shows part of a run the same day on the 12.50pm. Nine years later Ned Nelson was still driving though considerably over retiring age. Greatly disillusioned with continuing deterioration of the railway as compared with the days when he fired at Cookstown, he seemed to be of somewhat crusty temper to the latest brand of enthusiast who tended to presume much on a few moments' chat, and he had little patience either with the young firemen of the 'spoil' era. In 1959, however, Ned was still partial to fast running and here he was out to demonstrate that the black sheep *50* was able to match the best of her class.

Most younger readers will have no experience of steam mainline travel on a Sunday and even in 1959 possibilities had been almost reduced to summer trips to either Warrenpoint or Portrush. The scenery and locomotive variety of the former had undoubted appeal but for sheer performance the NCC 1pm to Portrush had great interest in that MPD units were not available for a 90min schedule, quite smart for three stops if more than a trivial load. Of the 1959 data I have, not all the runs were as good as an effort by Palmer with *10* the previous year when 79mph was attained at Dunadry. Indeed, neither Cole with *7*, R.W. Robinson with *57* nor Douglas with *54* during the earlier part of August managed to keep time. With eight bogies Magill was successful in an excellent run with *4* but Harris's run with *7* was the best of the lot, and the latter part of it is shown in Table E.

There were eight specials for the 12 August celebrations in Derry. For the first time tanks outnumbered moguls in the operation, Coleraine having *3*, *55* and *104* with Dunlop, Hayes and Elliott respectively. Bankhead and Scott had *1* and *7*, and the Belfast specials were worked by *57*, *95* and *99*, driven by Keenan, Nelson and Mahood. On 29 August every spare carriage was helping to run the RBP specials to Larne so the 1.50pm Antrim-Cullybackey consisted of *84* hauling a single railcar trailer, about 20 tons gross. The driver was Sam

McIlhagga, son of Bob, now retired. Arrival at Ballymena was dead on time on the 20min allowance from Antrim with three stops. 54mph before Cookstown Junction was brisk, even allowing for the trivial load, and 60mph on each of the next two sections was my last chance of recording a mile a minute with *84*. It was strange how every summer this connection continued to be given off the 1.10pm, apparently to serve Cookstown Junction and Kellswater, for I never saw more than a handful of passengers use it.

Early in September *95* was transferred to the Great Northern and a month later *94* came from the 'shops, followed by *54* in November. Eventually these two would also have to make the trip to Adelaide but in the meantime there were still nearly seventy GNR engines fit for UTA service, in addition to the six NCC engines transferred.

My last mainline experience of 1959 brought a comparatively new element into steam performance. On 14 November Palmer had *7* for a ten bogie football excursion to Coleraine and we had just got away to 67mph at Templepatrick when the communication cord was pulled. For the remainder of the journey and all the way back intermittent cord-pulling played havoc with timekeeping, completely spoiling what might have been yet another favourable entry in the records of this engine.

1960

Although they did not materially affect the NCC for some time and then only in a very limited way, this seems the time to mention the arrival from Manorhamilton of the last two SL and NCR locomotives to be built. In January they were bought by the UTA for £735 each and put into running order at Adelaide, where they were more in need of a 0-6-4 shunting tank than York Road would ever be again. Though the last to reach the Sligo Leitrim *Lough Melvin* was first into UTA service, numbered *26*. The other, *Lough Erne*, *27*, is still steamed from time to time at Whitehead by members of the Railway Preservation Society of Ireland of which her

167

owner, Roy Grayson, was for a period chairman. Beyer
Peacock engines of 1949 (delivered 1951), they weighed
55 tons 7cwt and had 4ft 8in driving wheels with cylinders
18in x 24in, the latter being an NCC standard of the past, at
any rate.

As far as the NCC steam position was concerned there were
now only four engines outside power class E, these being the
last 4-4-0s (*74* at Coleraine and *80* at Belfast) *13* and *19*. The
Kilrea goods had ceased operation in September and, apart
from the Larne line, which could still produce three to four
steam passenger trains in one day, there was really only the
Ballymena engine, which paid a visit to Antrim and worked
the Aldergrove train.

On 18 February during a heavy snowfall *94* was badly
derailed at the south end of Coleraine loop and *2* went down
with the breakdown crane. This unit was in considerable
demand at this period as Dunsilly bridge (No 82) was being
raised for the convenience of double-decker buses. Since that
time travelling fast here has given one the (doubtless erroneous) impression that the track is not safe.

On 11 March the 5.55am diesel had been derailed outside
Ballymoney by a sleeper, and it was considered that the
emergency brake had been unsatisfactory. The interest here
is that for the purpose of making a test, the identical cars (*47*
and *50*) and the same vans were assembled and hauled up to
Ballyclare Junction by *35*, the first GNR engine to have
heavy overhaul at York Road works. During the year a similar
engine, *33*, and two smaller 0-6-0s, *48* and *49*, also received
heavy repair. The GNR people were, in fact, asking for more
NCC engines, and at length *57* was permitted to go, not an
excessively generous gesture as this engine had a big mileage
done and was soon back on the NCC to go into the 'shops.

The steam situation at this period is best illustrated by the
working of a 8.50am special to Derry on 26 March, for which
104 had been selected. Inspector Hanley had examined this
engine at Ballymena a few days previously, finding her tubes
and firebox reasonably satisfactory and arranging for the

renewal of the brake blocks, a lubricator and the brick arch. On the actual day, a few minutes at Glarryford to cross the up express found the left large end heating a little and a broken pony spring. News of this was phoned to Derry, where *6* was found to be in steam. However, she had not sufficient coal to take her even to Coleraine and Derry's supply of pony springs had not been renewed. Despite the latter it was agreed that driver Heffron keep *104* for the trip back, which was in fact made without mishap despite the pony spring. Inspector Sherrard at Derry was a lively character, renowned for a very independent attitude to any kind of instruction from Belfast. An example of this occurred later in the year on 2 July when *104* was not lit up as instructed for the 3.15pm so that *4*, due there with the 12.50pm at 3.13pm, had to work this train. Dan O'Kane and Davis wasted little time with the changeover, not even turning the engine.

A character from the good old days was in the news on 28 March when Davie Brangam, noted for fast and not entirely accurate stops, had a mishap in Coleraine goods yard. *5* was shunting 22 wagons (loaded mostly with artifical manure) and the stop-block was struck severely and damaged, the bottom stop rail being broken. There was, however, no damage to engine or wagons. The resultant inquiry produced a wonderful collection of explanations and excuses; that, for instance, the rails were greasy after a slight drizzle of rain, that there was no light on the stop-block and that it had been damaged anyway sometime previously.

On Easter Monday *94* paid one of her last visits to Portrush and the following day no less than eight tanks were involved in 'demonstration' specials on the Larne line. Then on 6 May UTA steam facilities received prominence, for a change, when there was a newspaper account of the hire of *6* by a visiting Canadian called Timothy Eaton, who fancied a footplate trip to Ballymena, the engine crew being 'Gunboat' Smith and Tommy Freeborn. Ten years later the Chief Executive of NIR received similar publicity for another kind of trans-Atlantic deal, when 2-6-4 tank injectors were sold to an American steam society.

169

The summer timetable, from 13 June, produced a welcome amount of mainline steam on Saturdays, even if some of it was intended for July and August only. In addition to trains to Portrush at 9.25am, 1.10pm, 2.10pm and 2.55pm the 8.35am to Derry was steam and also the 5.55am and 12.50pm, though rostered for diesel. *55* was now on the GNR and *94*, after working the 8.35am on 25 June, went to Adelaide the following week. Visits were made to the NCC by two GNR moguls during the summer, *95* being at Portrush on 2 July with an excursion and *97* having a short spell at the 'shops to deal with slack tyres.

10 was the engine in Derry for the annual holiday week and on 4 August was employed testing tablet catchers over the single line. This showed the usual care to ensure unimpeded progress for the 'Apprentice Boys' specials to Derry. A slight handicap in the testing was that *10*, as well as having very thin tyres, was rather down on the axle boxes but nevertheless Glarryford, Dunloy and Macfin, noted currently for tablet misses, had their catchers adjusted. Only two of the specials on the day, 13 August, had moguls. Mahood and Mitchell had *104*, in good steaming form. The tank which piloted her to Kingsbog ran as usual onto the Ballyclare branch, the points of which then jammed, more than cancelling out the help she had given. The other mogul, *99*, was in the hands of Jimmy Keenan and R.J. Simpson. On the return trip they were handicapped with a useless right injector, normally a valuable asset in a mogul, but apparently in this case not even connected with the tender.

104 was in action again the following Saturday on the 12.50pm when Steenson was probably having his last chance to test a mogul with his old mate's standard of perfection of 14min for the 15.9 miles from Doagh to Kellswater. Racing along at 75mph did not seem to make proportionally worse *104*'s usual deafening rattle and severe vibration at 50mph and he seemed happy with a time of 14min 9sec. The Coleraine–Derry part of this run and another with *8* on a relief, run·for passengers off the Ardrossan boat, are shown in Table M. Johnny Kelly tended to work an engine too easily for time-keeping but the same table has a tolerable run with 99, probably the mogul which performed most regularly of the class over this stretch. These were her last days at Waterside but up to four years later Derry folk could still observe her from time to time on GNR goods into Foyle Road.

On 16 September 99 made a surprising appearance on the 5.30pm to Larne Harbour, from which she had to return, of course, tender first. A week later she went to the GNR to replace 95, withdrawn from service with a faulty tubeplate, final mileage being 1,159,274. A few weeks before 6 had been a rather surprising choice for the GNR.

The official attitude towards Portrush was now clearly to relegate it to be a 'summer only' branch line. Towards the end of August severe flooding caused some havoc on the branch, nor was morale thereon improved by the removal of the fine roofing over the platforms, so that Charlie Morrow, that energetic man in the signal cabin, may have felt glad that he was retiring from it all. From 3 October a bus replaced all train services on the Portrush branch. Needless to say, when it had to be re-opened next spring a tremendous amount of pw work was suddenly decided upon, with much overtime and Sunday work, all of which gave the impression that the idea now was to make the losses even more striking than before the intervening cheaply run bus period.

14 had been the last engine to penetrate the Draperstown branch and on 29 September 13 made a last trip to Randalstown, to collect eighteen cattle trucks and a van, which were left in an Antrim siding. The NCC working to Aldergrove had ceased with the end of the passenger services on the Antrim branch on 10 September. Thus the NCC main line was now completely without branch connections, where once a passenger could have deviated onto eight different branches.

The last weekend of October saw the retirement of fitter Bob Sloane at Ballymena and that anxious looking little Coleraine driver, Sammy Hayes. At the same time 93 emerged from the 'shops with yet another transfer emblem on her side.

171

The first had been the impressive LMS one followed by the not unattractive 'Red Hand' about the meaning of which no expert interpretation was required. The new affair was typically complicated and the cost of research prior to its production might well have repaired at least one steam engine.

On Saturday evening, 19 November, driver T.J. McAuley of the Belfast top link was run down and killed by MED units 10/11, working the 5.35pm from York Road to Whitehead. This train had left from No 4 platform and passed up the middle siding to reach the main down line, a procedure adopted by very few trains. It was presumed that McAuley had been struck from behind as he walked along the siding but the exact circumstances, or the reason for his apparent carelessness, were never fully explained. Few NCC drivers had handled passenger trains in a more competent or confident manner.

On 19 December 5 caused another investigation when Matt Harbinson broke Macfin gates with the 7am goods (eleven wagons and brake) ex Coleraine. Although this engine had been booked for defective brakes a few days previously, tests failed to show exactly why they had failed to act properly and there was some criticism of the driver for not whistling a warning to guard Speers Wiseman that he required assistance in stopping the train against adverse signals.

1961

99 had been sent off to the GNR rather optimistically the previous September with a twenty-year-old boiler so it was not surprising that she was soon back at York Road. However, the two moguls which mysteriously went back into service over the winter period, *93* and *98*, did so with two even older boilers, those which had originally come with *99* and *100* in 1938-39. So the UTA, with one eye on possible GNR closures and the other on the purse, were now really scraping the bottom of the barrel. For *99* they now went back to *93*'s 1942 boiler, with which, indeed, *99* produced some excellent work in due course on the GNR.

19 would now appear occasionally at Adelaide, to balance which *24*, a GNR 0-6-4 tank, originally *166*, could be seen frequently shunting Whitla Street goods yard. It was at the engine shunting York Road passenger yard that one mainly looked these days, for invariably this would be one of a most regular flow of outshopped engines (the most active for five years) and paint was not being spared. Up until the summer holiday at the works no less than ten engines had been turned out: three 0-6-0s, *32, 38* and *45* (each of a different class) two 4-4-0s, *62* and *63*, and five NCC engines.

Apart from a couple of Antrim-Ballymena locals there was almost no possibility of steam passenger on the NCC mainline till the Sunday School excursions of midsummer and then the summer timetable itself. This differed little from the previous year, although a new 9.40am to Derry during July and August was rostered for steam. A disappointment, to balance this, was that the Sunday afternoon 'express' no longer produced a steam engine, though one still could reach Portrush by steam on a Sunday, by the 9.40am. The through Derry-Larne Harbour train once again appeared for summer weekdays and worked by steam.

It was gratifying to observe heavy trains being provided for the steam turns so that easier timings still required interesting work by the tanks. On 15 July, for instance, Hugh O'Neill had *52* for ten bogies and a van, piloted to Kingsbog by *1*, and even that Sunday 9.40am had nine bogies for Joe Wilmont with *52* on 16 July, and for Jim Simpson with *3* on 6 August, all three runs producing 75mph at Dunadry.

50 had now gone to the GNR, but *51*, after returning for a visit to the works, began to do NCC mainline work for the first time, having been shedded at Larne for the nine years prior to going to Adelaide. *53* was outshopped in time for the August traffic and was at least blowing off at 200lb, whereas most of the other tanks, and especially those due for 'shops such as *7, 8* and *52*, were trying to do the job on 180lb. Coal too was consistently bad this summer, being mainly slack, though every time I observed *3* that summer she seemed to be bursting with steam. The self-cleaning smokeboxes of these engines meant, of course, that no longer did crews dread the job of cleaning the fire after a long trip with bad Scotch coal. For the old hands the standard of perfection had always been the genuinely blue Welsh variety, Joe Gallagher having on one occasion fired *97* from Larne Harbour to Derry and back again, via the Derry Central, without having to clean the fire, despite a very heavy train. If the next generation had things easier there was still a certain competence about a situation on a 1961 Sunday evening at Portrush where at 6.30pm the fireman of *51* for the 7.5pm was fast asleep with his fire banked up, but at 7.4pm precisely the engine blew off.

The 7.30pm ex Portrush had been smartened up to a commendable 90 minute schedule with two intermediate stops a couple of years previously, but invariably heavy excursion traffic spoiled the running of this train, the occasion in August 1959 when Jim Simpson reached Belfast to time with *95* and ten bogies being a rather rare one. So my 1961 experiences of this train was one only, with *4* giving Heffron some trouble, but a fast finish made him only 1min late into Belfast. Bankhead was another man, with experience of the narrow gauge, whose method of constantly opening and closing the regulator when driving the tanks had little traditional NCC acumen about it. However, the Ballymena driver did produce a good example of *51*'s steaming powers when he had 320 tons past milepost 50 in 6¾min from Ballymoney with the 3.15pm on 8 July.

104 had come from the 'shops in June and spent most of the summer on a fairly obvious duty for her, the 5.55am through to Derry, returning with the 1pm. However, Table J shows a run on the 3.25pm ex Portrush, in which her time of 80min from Portstewart with two further stops could be assessed as equal to those 80min timings of Portrush excursions before the war. *104* was not in existence to ever experience this kind of thing so it seems apt, on this her last NCC summer, to give this example.

It is worth reflecting at this point that *96* was the engine exchanged with the GNR in 1935, that *91* was the one sent in 1959 for regular involvement on express trains there and that only when no other mogul was left was *104* allowed to go. Here, I think, is NCC pride in their engines truly epitomised. At the time *96* was the newest engine they had except *97*, not properly run in. When I analyse my own runs carefully it seems clear that *91*, though neither as fast nor indeed as reliable as several of the other moguls, was consistently best for sustained tractive effort such as required for the Kellswater–Kingsbog section, a feature likely to suit much of the Great Northern main line. No NCC man had a good word to say about *104*, least of all in 1961.

By the end of the summer *6* had returned from the GNR to precede *4* into the 'shops, and *53*,.*54* and *104* all went over instead. *57* had already returned there after repair making a total of 12 out of 20 in all since 1952. Before the end of the year York Road works also turned out three more GN 0-6-0s after repair and *60*, *Slieve Donard*. *74*'s only surviving sister *80* was withdrawn in November and sold the following month for scrap, together with *15*, *72*, *84* and *96*, leaving twenty-nine NCC locomotives against the 1948 figure of sixty-six.

Before concluding the 1961 story, the week's tour of Irish railways, organised jointly by the IRRS, SLS and RCTS, should be mentioned in so far as it briefly affected the NCC. On 10 June *74*, as clean as York Road could manage, worked a special, tender first, to Greenisland, and then via the 'back line' to Antrim. It was fitting that Jimmy Keenan should be *74*'s driver as far as Antrim where *Lough Erne*, *27*, took over for a run over the Great Northern branch.

CHAPTER 8

By Accident or Design:1962-5

It is impossible not to feel some sympathy for the motive power folk of the UTA in 1959. They had just matured a scheme for complete dieselisation of what was left of the NCC and BCDR, and they now found themselves landed with GNR responsibility. Had the Ulster Government, upon whom they were dependent, now launched out into diesel expenditure for the GN section it might have solved their problem but the civil servants' remedy was simply to close a further 85 miles as soon as possible. In the meantime, therefore, the only solution was overhaul of a large number of steam engines.

One real benefit from this was that York Road could still be supplied with the steam power for the heavy summer traffic, which the 'not a puff' theorists seemed to have forgotten about. What is difficult to decide now is the exact motivation for the boiler renewals about to be mentioned in this chapter. Would these have been done but for the uncertainty about the future of the GN section? How otherwise could the UTA have coped with traditional summer Portrush traffic or did they just hope it would gradually fall off? Would the spoil project ever have materialised but for this 1962-65 boiler work?

It was some consolation to steam enthusiasts, at any rate, that NCC engines were providing plenty of excitement on foreign track, even if the NCC itself had become for the major part of the year almost as much like a tramway as the Bangor line.

1962

Steam engines could still be seen shunting at Derry, Ballymena and Larne, though the latter shed was now closed, the engine coming down each morning with the 5.20am goods. It was a very busy day when there was more than 150 miles of steam on the NCC. To get this situation in the correct perspective it should be remembered that even for some time afterwards the Kings were still thumping big Paddington trains up Hatton bank and the Gresley pacifics still had it mostly their own way on the east-coast main line. But in seven years' time, where any of these BR engines still survived, it was in the hands of preservation societies with no chance of performing in ordinary service, whereas even as late as 1969 the NCC tanks were called upon to work heavier mainline passenger trains than ever before.

Since 1959 the NCC tanks would be doing well to average 20,000 miles a year, except those on the GNR which were clocking up half as much again. During 1960 the top NCC engine was *55* with 37,296 miles and again, with 33,084, this engine was second only to *57* with 35,831 the following year. The mogul which ran most over these two years was *93* with 32,590 in 1961 and these three engines were all, of course, on the GNR section, where there was to be even more activity in 1962 with *53* with 36,747 miles just fractionally ahead of *57, 54* and *50*. In 1961 no tank based solely on the NCC had run more than the 24,928 miles of *52*. It was interesting how the newer engines were being used more, as if to bring up all the mileages to a similar point, which they were now all approaching, when the fireboxes could not last much longer.

During March the monotony of the 2-6-4 tank type was being ameliorated slightly, not only by the persistent presence of *13* shunting in the goods yard, but by the sight of VS 4-4-0 *58* over from the GNR for firebox repair. NCC enginemen pondered on the possible appetite for coal which this vast boiler might produce. The powers that be had no doubt that, obnoxious as NCC steam engines undoubtedly were, this GNR example was even worse.

Good Friday produced in the morning a dull run by John Moore with *8* on a boat relief to Derry and then in the evening the fine run with *1* shown in Table A. Jimmy Ramsey was still living in Larne and indeed he had fired on *8* there for nearly a decade. It was possibly his anxiety to gain a lift at Ballymena on a lorry over to Larne, despite a late start, which motivated such fine running, which should easily have produced an 'eighty' but for the pw slack after Ballymartin gates.

The Sunday School traffic in May and June proved to be at least as heavy as ever and got the tanks into form for the summer timetable. On 4 May, for example, there were specials at 9.35am and 9.45am from York Road and 11.5am from Ballymena as well as two from the GNR. The staff at Portrush, who plastered the return carriages with large paper reservation notices year after year, must have become very familiar with such gospel halls as Harryville, Monkstown and Cloughfern, with Ferndale Mission House, and churches such as St Augustine (Derry), St Patrick's (Ballymena) and First Bally-macarrett (Belfast).

Three GN 0-6-0s (*43,44* and *47*) were repaired during the spring as well as two small 4-4-0s, *66* and *68*, getting preference over two tanks, *7* and *9*, overdue for repair. *56* had come from the GNR for overhaul and when this was done she stayed at York Road for the summer. The new timetable contained nothing revolutionary. The 1½ hour timing of the 7.30pm had ceased due to a stop at Cullybackey and the 3.15pm ex Derry was altered to 3pm, running into York Road instead of Larne Harbour.

They were trying a 1.40pm departure for Sunday half-day excursionists to Portrush (it had been 2pm in 1955). There was nothing of great note about the performances by *56* on 26 July nor by *4* the following Sunday, and *1*, on the last Sunday in August, was 17min late into Portrush on a 93min

178

timing, after some delays en route. If Jack McAuley (son of
T.J.) had run all the way with *1* as he did over the
Ballymoney-Coleraine section he could have recovered some
time. With six bogies these 8.3 miles were run in the smart
time of 9min 49sec, maximum 71mph.

Carson had been a significant name in Ulster political life.
Bill, that stout Ballymena driver, whose rather unctuous
voice had seemed so out of place on a run-down 4-4-0, had
been a reliable performer during the fifties, and the bare-
headed fireman of Ramsey's run with *1* on 20 April had been
John Carson, a very capable chap, today driving diesels
on the remains of his native BCDR. Ned Carson had fired to
Fillis at Coleraine for many years and on 4 August he turned
up driving the 2.10pm Belfast-Portrush. A footplate passenger reported *3* as very loose in the boxes but steaming reasonably. Carson, apparently, pulled her up to 5%, which takes
some believing, though there was certainly that complaining
hiss off the relief valves on the cylinders and even the downhill
work was rather poor.

A run with another young Coleraine driver appears in Table
N. Jim Coulter had been one of that group of large and robust
looking firemen there, which also included Houston, McNabb
and Swann. Here was an example of a fireman copying his
driver's style, for Hughie McDonnell had run better than most
when he had a good engine. Elliott at Coleraine based his
style more on Johnny McAuley, I think, than Piggot, but
Dunlop certainly resembled his old partner, Billy McDonald,
in his attitude towards driving. Anyway, this was his last year
on regular footplate work as he succeeded Hanley as locomotive inspector early the following year.

6 monopolised the heavy 8.35am this summer, the greatest
load being on 11 August when she had eleven bogies and a
van, piloted to the summit by *8*. A fortnight later it was like
old times to see a mogul on a Derry train at this time of the
morning, though in fact *93* was an engine seldom seen on the
8.25am in the good old days. This engine remained overnight
at Coleraine, working back the 8.20pm ex Portrush on Sunday

night. With only five bogies Cole did not have to exert *93* for an early arrival at Belfast. It was most fitting that my last NCC mogul run should be with a driver who had handled them so long with affection and dignity. *98* also made a brief NCC appearance with a 'Covenant' special on 29 August when *3, 4, 6* and *8* were also so engaged.

For a football special to Coleraine on 24 November and again on a boat relief to Derry on 22 December it was the same driver, 'Gunboat' Smith. The engines were respectively *6* and *7* and the only statistic worth mentioning was a smart time of 24min 22sec by *7* from Ballymena to Ballymoney with eight bogies. While steam was thus creeping quietly back into winter mainline operations another GNR 0-6-0, *34*, was outshopped and then in December the last blue engine to have heavy repair at York Road, *67*.

1963

The workshops at York Road continued to be busy, as NCC engines which had been employed for some time on the Great Northern were now coming back for repair. Thus in the first four months of this year, *91, 54, 50* and *57* were all dealt with, in addition to another GNR 0-6-0, *35*. Easily the most interesting item here was that *50* had got a new firebox in the boiler off mogul *99*, the original boiler, in fact, of *101* (1939). This was a most portentous event as not since the winter of 1954 had an NCC engine been given a new firebox. True, the age of the actual boiler did not seem to look too far into the future, though in fact seven years later it was still in use. An interesting point is that *50* was in age the eleventh of the tanks, but the first to have its boiler taken out. It was thus certainly not decided by mileage done, for even *51* and *52* had more run at that time, though, of course, all the tanks were already over the 400,000 miles regarded on the NCC as the maximum life of a firebox. There seems just a possibility that *50* was chosen because she had always been the most troublesome, though indeed a serious flaw may have been detected.

When they did get round to repairing a tank for NCC work it was *2*, which had, in fact, spent some of the winter on the GNR section. This pet engine of York Road had certainly been a surprising transfer, which came to an abrupt conclusion on 5 February at Lisburn when a local train, composed appropriately enough of diesel units *6* and *7*, loaned also from the NCC, was run into by *2*, heading the evening train to Dublin. The engine sustained considerable damage to her smokebox and pony truck but there were no serious casualties. Probably nearly due for overhaul anyway, this accident obviously accelerated it and *2* was in service again on 1 June, but never again, I'm sure, the excellent engine she had been for the first dozen years of her life.

During the early part of the year the 5.30pm to Larne Harbour was frequently steam, *52* and every one of Nos *1-10* being used except *4, 6* and *9*. From the advent of the summer timetable both this and the 5pm were officially booked for steam, the 5.30 engine usually returning with the goods, and the shunting engine with the 7pm passenger. On Saturdays (the busy day on the main line) the only booked Larne line steam was the 12.35pm perishable ex Larne Harbour returning at 4pm, an engine being obtained for this by the simple expedient of cancelling the 7.25pm goods on Friday nights. York Road generally arranged it that the 5.30pm on Friday nights had their most troublesome engine, one which would not have been much use on the main line anyway.

During most of this period an engine lay dead at Coleraine during the week, though available for ballasts as required. On Saturdays it was actively employed taking the through carriages to Portrush off the 8.35am ex Belfast and had further branch trains at 10.18am and 8.29pm. Saturday steam from Belfast, apart from the 8.35am, was officially only during July and August, at 5.55am and 9.40am to Derry and 2.10pm to Portrush. The engine of the 9.40am was booked to work the 3pm ex Derry as far as Coleraine, where it then lay overnight to work the 7.30pm Portrush-Belfast, now the only Sunday steam train.

York Road evidently felt that eleven engines was not quite enough so they borrowed 55 from Adelaide, though by now this engine was in a fairly rundown condition. Amongst what they already had 5 was the worst, being fit for little but shunting, though she did manage that Saturday Larne job at a couple of busy weekends. Of more interest was the use of *33* (class SG3 0-6-0) on this perishable turn on 27 July while she was running in after her second overhaul at York Road. This meant that the previous day she had been an amazing sight on the 5.30pm express to Larne Harbour, but this was not the first NCC passenger train *33* had worked, for the previous Saturday Ballymena had used her for their 'star' turn, that one-carriage 1.50pm from Antrim to Cullybackey, which somehow or other still survived. Of the performance the only data I have to hand is that John Scott reached Cullybackey from Ballymena in 7min 38sec with the 18 ton load of a sparsely loaded railcar trailer, 40mph being attained.

With its cross channel traffic to Portrush, Derry and Donegal the 8.35am ex Belfast continued to be the most important mainline train. On nine occasions between 22 June and 31 August ten bogies were provided, usually with a van as well at the front for newspapers etc. A nonstop timing of 42min was not unduly generous with these big trains, even though a pilot could usually be found to assist to the summit, the Ballymena pilot later adding power in the rear for the climb to Galgorm gates. For the recorder of performance a happy variety was provided during this period, no less than eight different engines being used, *9* and *10* twice and *1, 2, 6, 7, 8* and *55* once each. *2* was fresh from the 'shops in June but played a very modest part in the summer's activities in which *7* and *9* were the outstanding performers. When *10* appeared early in August with *50*'s boiler and a new firebox York Road seemed to be getting some consideration at last, but this engine, reckoned by some drivers to be the liveliest of the class a few years ago, seemed now terribly weak on the banks though swift enough down hill.

Out of so much 8.35 data I shall have to restrict myself to

a few runs, only one of which appears in the tables. This was Mahood in charge of 9 on 22 June 1963 (Table M), even though the Coleraine–Derry section can be no one's choice as the most exciting part of the main line, especially in this direction. The most notable part was the fast time to milepost 93, the best in the table, which should have brought 9 into Derry in record time from Limavady Junction, despite quite a slow start. However, no doubt Mahood had very little experience of this part of the road and carefully observed the restrictions outside Derry. The following week McAuley had 1 and ran in from a stop at Eglinton (to leave off the water can) in 10min 55sec, a smart effort which included a speed of 64mph.

Out of Belfast two ten bogie runs considerably bettered any of the others. On 10 August Jackie Bell had 7, with the aforesaid John McAuley assisting to Kingsbog with 55. Bell was by this time quite experienced in NCC type operations, otherwise he would hardly have been working a big train into Derry on the occasion of the annual visit of the Apprentice Boys, when any kind of error could bring chaos (and shame and disgrace) amidst the intensive railway activity around the Maiden City. 7 reached Ballymena in 40min 9sec that day, just 11 seconds better than a run with Jimmy Simpson a fortnight later when 2 was piloted to Kingsbog by 7. An interesting feature of 7's run on 10 August was that after three Portrush carriages had been detached, as usual, at Coleraine, the train pulled forward and three carriages *from* Portrush and full of Apprentice Boys were added to the rear, the signalman having a long walk to deliver the tablet. 55 worked the 9.40am the same day to Derry and they got rid of her on the 1pm, which on this big day has traditionally been used to expel the engine most likely to upset the homeward procession later on. The other engines in Derry that day on specials were 2, 4, 6, 8, 9, 10 and 52. 9 returned on the 3pm ordinary train, 7 taking her place on one of the return specials.

The 1pm ex Derry had always seemed the Cinderella of the NCC main line from good days prior to 1957 when a Coleraine Castle worked out at 1.10pm, until modern times when one could stand down near Doagh in the valley of the Sixmile-water, observe a vast slow trail of blue smoke and discover in the end that it wasn't a steam engine after all but MPD cars rather overloaded and heating up increasingly as Belfast slowly approached. Activities between Derry and Coleraine tended to be impromptu at the best of times and especially with this train. On 22 June *9* left Derry with eight bogies and two vans, an unusually heavy load. Although booked to stop at Eglinton the train passed through and then spent no less than 19¾min at Limavady Junction. This was because someone had at last realised that the weekly notice instruction about retaining three bogies at Derry had been ignored. These carriages were now left off at the junction, by which time the 11.25am diesel ex Belfast, running very late, was in the section. Even after all this a special stop was made at Magilligan for parcels.

With this train on 10 August whilst passing through Cullybackey at 63mph *55* collected the tablet but did not discharge the one from Glarryford. Driver Hugh O'Neill, seeing the tablet in fireman Simpson's hand, did not at first realise the situation and the train was over two level crossings before it could be stopped and reversed. This had been the engine on 28 July for the Sunday 8.30pm ex Portrush, which did not appear in the public timetable, being an idea, on certain Sundays, to give day trippers a longer day in Portrush despite that resort's reputation for chilly evenings, even in the height of summer.

On 11 August the outward excursion at 1.20pm was diesel but an interesting series of events produced steam again on the 8.30pm special. Mahood and McAtamney travelled down to Coleraine that afternoon to work the 7.30pm ex Portrush with the engine stabled there over night. They found both *1* and *6* in the shed but the young lad entrusted with the job of lighting up *1* had made a sorry mess of it. The crew found him not far from tears as he poured oil into a firebox crammed full of Welsh slack.

So the fire was now relit with a few bits of timber and Portrush was contacted with instructions to send the excursion diesel on the ordinary 7.30 in the hope that *1* might just be ready for the 8.30pm. Then a typical complication of the sixties was revealed. Very few compartments in the original 7.30 set had lights, its comparatively early arrival into Belfast having been taken into account. For a time it seemed a real possibility that a three-car MED set in Coleraine yard might have to be used, with *1* working the 7.10am next morning, but suddenly, in a manner reminiscent of that June afternoon in 1958, *1* began to make steam. In due course, despite an extra stop, the special ran into York Road only 1min late.

Again this year 'enthusiasts' were responsible for a 4-4-0 having a run down the NCC main line. *174* , ex GNR S class, with a BCDR driver (Table G) did not make quite as impressive a comparison with average NCC performance as sister engine *171* was to do as late as 1970. In this respect it shows the paucity of outside interest during the thirties that another engine of this class, *170*, then in her unrebuilt state, covered 1853 NCC miles in a week (in exchange for mogul *96*) without anyone having any record of her actual performance.

When *97* and *49* were outshopped in October and November respectively they were the last mogul and then the last GNR engine to receive heavy repair at York Road. *48* had proceeded *49* in the works and *5* had also reappeared, now with a new firebox in the boiler off *10*. Her own boiler was now available to take a new firebox for *3*, which went into the 'shops. *52* was also overhauled in November, retaining the same boiler and firebox. Unfortunately this meant that a splendid engine missed her chance of being one of the lucky eleven to survive into the spoil age. On 21 December she went to Derry with a pre-Christmas boat relief. As far as Ballymena, at least, this was probably the best down run of the year, meriting a place in Table B. Despite an easier timing and a considerably heavier train Steenson so much improved on his *104* performance that he exactly equalled the Doagh-Kellswater time of a much lighter North Atlantic Express run, in the same table.

185

1964

As far as NCC steam was concerned this year took a very similar path to 1963. Nevertheless at the quieter times of the year the religion of dieselisation was being implemented in a number of small ways. The economics of this depend upon how one considers a costly MPD unit compares with a run down steam engine as shunter of Derry goods yard. Similar units now worked all NCC goods trains, except those on the Larne line.

On the GN section, *97*, assisted by *91, 94* and *99*, was now monopolising the goods workings on the other route to Derry, as well as a few local passenger trains between Belfast and Portadown. *93* and *98* had now run their last mile, and observing *10* haul the King out of Whitehead shed the previous November, it had certainly not occurred to me that some part of her was for further use, but in due course, just in time for the end of the summer timetable, *51* was to be out-shopped with a new firebox in *98*'s boiler. In January *8* and then *1*, the following month, were sent for their first experience of the Wellington bank and, although neither was in very good ·shape, some surprisingly good work was done. In May, *53* was outshopped with a new firebox in *3*'s boiler and in surprisingly quick time the discarded boiler had in turn received a new firebox and been given to *55*.

Easter came early and produced a reasonable amount of steam activity at Portrush. *52* worked the 9.25am, returning in the evening with the 7.30pm. Shades of spoil train drivers of the future were reflected in the enginemen involved: McGarvey firing to Mitchell on the 9.25 and McDonald to Shannon on the 7.30pm. Another engine in good condition, *5*, had a 9.45am special to Portrush, returning at 6.45pm. *6* worked the 4.5pm to Larne and *3* shunted in the passenger yard. Tuesday, as usual, was a little more active, with *10* on a 10.15am special to Portrush. *5* and *52* were on the same trains as the previous day and *3* took empty carriages to Portrush for a special back at 7.40pm.

The summer timetable was faced with only nine tanks now on the NCC, of which *4* and *6* were in pretty poor shape. The heaviest steam train in the country continued to be the 8.35am on Saturdays. *9* and *10* each worked it three times during the summer timetable of eleven weeks. The best 8.35 nonstop time to Ballymena this year was by a fairly recent addition to the drivers' ranks at York Road. Crawley's experience of tank engines can not have been very great but with *3* on 27 June he reached Ballymena in 40min 6sec, the nine bogies and van being piloted to the summit by *10*. Just as commendable, however, was a time of 41min 14sec by Sloane with *52* for a vast train of eleven bogies and van, for which *4* was the pilot to Kingsbog.

To facilitate daily travels to the Magherafelt area Crawley's everyday duties were principally involved with the workings of coal and pulp specials to Courtaulds siding at Mount, operated conveniently in the middle of the day. It was, in any case, quite good policy to have a regular crew on this job, as the steeply graded sidings had their problems. On Saturdays, however, Alfie was usually free for the occasional 'enthusiasts' special and in particular was a familiar figure on the footplate of GS & WR *186* a few years later. An interesting engine used for one of these specials in 1964 was former GN 4-4-0 *202* (now numbered *67*). There was nothing very startling about a time of 31min 50sec nonstop from York Road to Antrim with three bogies, but 64mph was a tolerable maximum speed to record for a new class down Dunadry bank.

Ever since the wholesale sacking of firemen (in 1960) had not been justified by an equal amount of dieselisation (except possibly for a short theoretical period) the finding of sufficient crews to work steam specials on busy days had become a major headache. Should a fireman not turn up (an increasing hazard under modern conditions), carrying through the day's timetable could become very difficult, rather a pity with engines capable of doing much more work. The day after the traditional 'Twelfth' holiday had always been a big day for Portrush and it is interesting to examine, from the following list, the organising skill behind NCC arrangements to provide, with steam, a truly Gargantuan service. We see here York Road making use of five Coleraine enginemen (Edgar, Allen, Cairns, Friel and McConnell) to help work their specials.

14 July 1964

		Driver	Fireman	Engine No.
8.55am special	Belfast–Portrush	S. Sloane	W.J. Gillespie	2
9.25am	Belfast–Portrush	P. Shannon	R.J. Simpson	10
9.40am special	Belfast–Portrush	A. McLean	J. Cairns	9
10.25am special	Belfast–Portrush	S. Edgar	S. Friel	52
11.10am special	Belfast–Portrush	J. McAuley	D. McDonald	5
Light engine	Coleraine–Derry	D. O'Kane	J. Craig	9
Standby or shunt	Ballymena till 3.30pm	D. McKeown	P. Dobbin	6
Standby or shunt	Ballymena till 10.30pm	J. Scott	J. McIlwaine	6
6.35pm special	Portrush–Belfast	J. Heffron	J.D. Kitchen	2
7.20pm special	Portrush–Belfast	J. Allen	W.J. McConnell	52
7.35pm special	Portrush–Belfast	W. Leathem	M. McClelland	5
8pm special	Portrush–Belfast	H. O'Neill	T.H. Ramsey	10
8.40pm special	Portrush–Belfast	P. Magill	W. McGarvey	3

Specials of more route interest were those traditionally on the last Saturday of June from Coleraine to Castlerock, worked this year by *4* and *10*, and two from the GNR section on 18 July, worked by *57* and *97*, the former engine turning up again the following Saturday. The operating department can scarcely have blessed the organisers of Chipperfield's circus for requiring a couple of very unusual looking specials on such a busy day as 11 July. *6* and *10* were the engines involved here. On 10 August seven steam specials arrived at Waterside with Apprentice Boys and an interesting aspect of this gathering in 1964 was that in this, the last summer of its existence, Foyle Road received three specials headed by NCC engines *53, 55* and *97*.

This was another summer full of good running. Freddie Mahon proved that a lively sprint with *52* on the 1.10pm was not a mere flash in the pan for he produced another brisk effort the very next week on the same train with 7. The big BCDR man, Robinson, with 74mph as early as Templepatrick with 9 on the 2pm on 18 July, had Kilmakee gates to blame for his failure to clock up an 'eighty'. This road crossing leads to the airport and the increasing traffic has fully justified Kilmakee being the first mainline crossing on the NCC to have, in August 1971, automatic half barriers erected. In trying to assess the merits of the various mogul tanks and in particular the first ten (most often used on the NCC) the student of performance is constantly finding outstanding runs by each in turn, making judgement of the relative brilliance of each a matter for endless argument . . . all, that is, except 5. This engine, of all the class, had been most snugly retained at the home shed of York Road and should have been the top engine. But looking for high speeds down past Dunadry or tremendous haulage efforts up through Doagh one looks almost in vain. However, on 5 September it was R.W Robinson, again, who brought her into the limelight. This run, in fact, is the best in Table M and the staff at Waterside must have rubbed their eyes to see the 8.35am rolling in ahead of time, despite the complication of picking up a pilotman.

Tables H and K show that an afternoon at Portrush hadn't spoiled Mahon's enthusiasm for timekeeping. It had been NCC practice at slack periods to give selected firemen experience in the workshops and Fred had been one of these so I had at times in the past regarded him more as a fitter than a driver. These efforts with 7 and 52 changed all that and are recollected with the greatest pleasure, not least because both engines were completely withdrawn the following year. However, during 1964 6 was in much worse shape than either of the engines she was eventually to outlive, which makes an exhibition of power on the 25 July with the 3pm ex Derry all the more commendable. The fact that driver Gordon Beggs had very little mainline experience was probably a blessing in disguise for one of the old drivers might well have refused an engine, which in addition to all the knockings and bangs and a bad blow in the firehole ring had one injector quite useless and a boiler blowing off at 180lb. Yet, with no less than 360 tons Ballymoney–Ballymena was run in 27¼min, fireman Harry Ramsey making skilful use of the one asset they had, excellent coal.

It should not be forgotten, before completing the story of 1964, that this was the year of the 'Grand Tour of Irish Railways' which affected the NCC in a rather more extensive way than the courtesy visit of 1961. *97* worked the special set of coaches from Great Victoria Street to York Road (a very familiar route for engines in NIR days) and, in retrospect, *7* was an excellent choice for a run to Larne Harbour and back. After that *97* took over again to cover the entire NCC mainline and Portrush branch.

1965

It was not really intended that the closures to reduce the Great Northern part of the UTA to one mainline should drag out till mid February. However, William Craig's anti-railway policy at Stormont saw another step of inevitable success on 13 February, with one steam shed only left on the GNR. (Adelaide), where for irregular requirements such as passenger excursion and ballast trains four recently shopped tanks were available as well as *50*. As soon as *54* got a new firebox in the boiler of *56* she returned to Adelaide.

At the beginning of the year York Road was down to its lowest ever stud of engines, for *2* and *7* also went to the GNR for the death agonies, leaving really only *3, 5* and *10* to cover ballasts and diesel failures until *4* was outshopped, also with a new firebox, *51*'s boiler being used. *6*, unfit for use, was about to go to the 'shops and *52* was stored at Coleraine. Apart from the three mogul tanks, the only other engine to get repair was *27*. Sister *26* took up a suggestive position outside the works as soon as *Lough Erne* emerged but W.A.G. Macafee happened to observe this further possibility of steam survival and is reported to have come down very firmly against having more

190

than one left of this type for such shunting and dock work as now remained.

It may be of interest at this stage to mention briefly the extent to which NCC fares had been increased, especially while Howden ('the public must be made to pay') was the UTA chairman. One could not, of course, expect to travel to Antrim for the third-class single fare of 10d of 1855 but a hundred years later it was only 2s 8d, still very reasonable and not greatly above the pre-war charge. However, by 1958 this had become 3s 4d, by 1961 3s 7d, and by 1965 4s 2d. Today it is the decimal equivalent of 5s 10d but apart from a recent panic due more to the loss of revenue from the 'spoil' contract than wage increases, the most rapid increase was during that period in the sixties when the public were 'conned' by some remarkable propaganda by which 'to be fair to everyone' almost all fares were considerably increased. The general idea was that there had been some anomalies (as, of course, there were) in that mileage was not strictly adhered to. A good idea of the fair and honourable way by which this was adjusted can be had when one discovers that the single fare to Whitehead (14¾ miles) from Belfast, was now to be the same as Antrim (19¼ miles). A more business-like attitude towards attracting the public came with Howden's successor and later, Northern Ireland Railways. If not as good value as the Runabout Tickets of the thirties, the 70s and later the 50s weekly tickets were nevertheless a very good buy. It is probably of little use to speculate whether the powers that be are aware that the great popularity of these tickets around the 1967 period had much more to do with the activities of NCC drivers on steam engines and especially the spare link at York Road than any new diesels or scenic delights of the dwindling railway scene in Northern Ireland. Certainly the figures for 1971 might make interesting comparison with those of 1966-8.

During the spring months *97* lay outside York Road works but the other moguls did not require any decision and were sold in May. *104*, with 830,133 miles, was the only one not to attain a million, of these final survivors, but even this was considerably more than the tanks, the first of which had arrived less than four years after *104*. A month before this *1* and *2* had returned from the GN section, but *7, 8, 9* and *50* lay out of steam at Portadown for some time before York Road began to think about them for the summer. *7* and *8* reached Adelaide during April, but only *8* made the further journey back to the NCC the following month and it was July before *9* reached York Road. *50* also came over for a few days but returned to Adelaide once the 12 August excitement was over. It was not so much that the latter depot had any possible use for her but rather that the myth was still being perpetuated that the NCC was a completely dieselised area on which steam locomotives would be unwelcome ornaments.

Faced with running to Dublin without tender engines Adelaide was presented with an old mogul tender, which when attached to the rear of tank engines could provide the additional coal and water needed, but airlocks were only one of the difficulties experienced when this was attached to *55*. As early as May the idea seemed to be abandoned and instead *54* and *55* had their bunkers built up to take more coal.

19 June was the first really big Saturday of the year at Portrush, which received no less than six tanks (*1, 2, 4, 5, 8* and *54*). The previous day *10* had worked the 5.35pm local train to Carrickfergus, a new steam duty this summer. This and the 5.30pm were the only Larne line duties officially booked for steam now that goods haulage had ceased. Of course steam continued to be used for the Courtaulds traffic, but the most significant sign was the frequent use of tanks on such Larne trains during the week as the 6.47am, 3.10pm and 5pm. It had ceased to be just a matter of lighting up engines on Saturday for Portrush.

The 1.10pm to Portrush, though rostered for and indeed operated by diesels during July and August, had *10* for both the last two Saturdays of June. This engine was still in good condition and lively in performance (Table G) blowing off at 210lb pressure. Probably it was *52*, however, and not the newly shopped engines *4* and *6*, which took most of the honours this summer, though *3*, too, produced her usual quota of good runs. Certainly *52*'s winter in Coleraine (she was not steamed till July) did not seem to have had the expected ill effects, though indeed she was suddenly withdrawn a few months later. It seems more likely that it was only by keeping her off almost daily use hammering up and down the Larne line that in the end enabled her firebox to survive over the summer period.

An interesting arrangement from 1st July provided an 8.50am to Derry, showing that the 8.35am was becoming too unwieldy to serve both Derry and Portrush. A reasonable idea now was that the refreshment car still went with the 8.35am Portrush as far as Coleraine, where it was attached to the 8.50am when it arrived. Much less reasonable were the ideas of the timetable people. With Templepatrick signal cabin now closed through lack of staff (they said) and another long section (Antrim–Ballymena) ahead it was asking for trouble to insert an Antrim stop into the 8.35am and then run a nonstop train to Ballymena 15min later. There was an air of desperation about such arrangements belonging to a very different railway from that of 1938. However, against this fall in white-collared morale a new generation of drivers was taking over. Men like Crymble, McAtamney and McGarvey, Rob Graham, Alan Robinson and R.J. Simpson were producing a very consistent standard of fast running which helped in great measure to compensate for what was clearly now a gradual rundown of the railway. The disastrous compensation scheme was resulting in a loss of trained staff, both valuable and disinterested, but resultant promotion had at least given this generation an earlier chance than their predecessors.

The previous summer's running had shown that it was fortunate for NCC performance that *52* had not joined the other seven later members of this class on the GN section. Yet it was more than one really expected to try out a new driver on the Sunday 7.30pm ex Portrush and experience the

N

fine run shown in Table H. A few days later on the weekday
7.30pm, loaded to nine bogies, Jimmy Semple ran from
Ballymoney to Cullybackey in 23min 51sec and was only
3 minutes late into Belfast. Semple, whose brother William
had been a regular sight in charge of *92* on the wartime Larne
Harbour–Derry boat train, could not by any stretch of the
imagination be called a steam enthusiast. Most of his railway
career had been as a fairly reluctant fireman on the Larne line,
but with *52*, on this his last summer before retirement, he
seemed suddenly to take on a new lease of life so that one
realised that he was a very capable driver. 'Steam is all right
when you have an engine like this,' he remarked after the run,
a moral victory for *52* over the MPD units.

No doubt some Coleraine men, with views very similar to
Semple's about steam, were far from pleased to find that
their rostered turn of the 7.30pm ex Portrush had invariably
a steam engine, though they got, of course, a diesel unit for
the 10pm back to Coleraine. Most of their driving with tanks
had been with the 1.5pm ex Derry until it was dieselised, the
standard of work for this being low compared to a heavy
7.30pm. Maybe too, sharing the footplate with a strange
young Belfast fireman was also responsible for some poor
efforts, though when one got a man with a good nerve, like
Coulter, there was at least a fast finish. On 24 July he was in
charge when I had my last mainline run with *8*, and his time
for ten bogies on the 7.30pm was 26min 13sec in from
Antrim with 71mph on Bleach Green viaduct and a time of
only 3min 19sec for the 4.1 miles from Monkstown to
milepost 2.

York Road works' last example of heavy repair, *6*, added
nothing to their good reputation. She was now very poor on
heavy trains, doubtless due to faulty valve setting, but nevertheless York Road insisted on turning her out for important
trains. In contrast *4* seemed since her visit to the works to be
now better than ever and it is a staggering job to try to recollect just how many occasions over the five years after January
1965 this engine has been involved in remarkable runs. It is

fortunate, therefore, that there was one run made by *4* at the end of this summer which not only must take prior place in that list but some might say was the finest NCC run ever made.

The data in Table I cannot do justice to the atmosphere of this run, with every additional irritating delay making a punctual arrival increasingly unlikely, until leaving Ballymena Alan had only 32½min remaining to reach Belfast and he was booked to *stop* at Antrim. Even with MPD units in top form most drivers might have settled for reaching Belfast at least 5min late. I do not know of 80mph being previously recorded in either direction between Ballymena and Antrim, and this run to Antrim in even time seems now almost unbelievable, though it was, in fact, recorded by a number of experienced (and deserving) 'timers'. *5* must have been doing quite well that day with the 3pm ex Derry but just catching her at Antrim advance starter cost *4* about ¾min, so a net time of 20¼ to Belfast seems fair.

With eleven tanks now usefully renewed with new fireboxes 1965 seemed to augur a more benevolent attitude on the part of the management not only towards steam, but for the future of the railway itself. A new idea about livery also seemed to indicate a renewal of interest and no one could complain about blue and cream for the GN section or olive green and cream for the Bangor line, in both cases showing some respect for past history. These sections of line had now no steam, of course, but on the NCC, which had, a new maroon livery, similar to the former LMS colour, was applied to diesel stock only. A few of the engines, such as *4, 6, 51* and *54* had still reasonably bright paintwork but the steam carri-ages, sombre enough at any time in that flat green, were now in strong contrast. Certainly at this period all the paint in the world could not disguise some very poor diesel performance.

One steam carriage which did receive the new maroon livery was *180*, former GNR *226*, a modern steam corridor first. On 13 September this vehicle and four others in drab UTA green reached Portrush with an enthusiasts' special hauled by *49* (formerly GNR *149*). The 1937 version of this class of 0-6-0s had been intended amongst other duties (it was said) for working excursion trains from the Portadown area via Cookstown to Portrush but there seems to be no data as to whether this was ever implemented.

CHAPTER 9

Indian Summer of a 2-6-4 Tank:1966-9

It could be said that none of the events which make up this part of the NCC main line's story would have taken place but for the Magheramorne spoil contract, twenty miles from that main line. Yet it is probably more accurate to suggest that just as Great Northern requirements provided a smoke screen to provide summer steam power for the dieselised NCC main-line for over six years, the spoil project ensured proper hand-ling of Portrush traffic without the railway having to admit that they actually depended upon steam for summer traffic, unless a further investment was made in more diesels. Certainly the boiler work on the tanks was begun before there was any talk of Magheramorne spoil, the contract for which was apparently secured by the new manager, John Coulthard. It was, however, his successor, Hugh Waring, who derived some prestige from a resultant profit for the NCC for the first time for twenty years. Carefully studied, his financial statement did reveal how completely this had depended upon those forty wagon trains, but there was no direct reference, of course, to the fact that 'outmoded' steam power had handled the job throughout.

1966

With the withdrawal of *2, 8* and *52* the NCC section began
this year with only seven tanks and it was not till June that
51 and *53* came over from the Great Northern, followed a
few weeks later by *50*. With *9* fit, apparently, for little more
than shunting, the other engines were kept busier, per engine,
than York Road had known for over six years. Even in January
most evenings had at least two steam workings to Larne and
as the year advanced the behaviour of the MED units, in particular, became increasingly suspect, for apart from failures
they were involved in several derailments. By May things had
deteriorated still further so that six Larne line trains were
officially rostered for steam for a couple of weeks, *4* and *6*
bore the brunt of this though *1, 3, 5* and *10* were also used.

On 28 May the Sunday School season was in full spate with
3, 4, 6, 51 and *53* all visiting Portrush, the last two on
Portadown specials. The following Saturday entirely different
engines were provided, with *1, 5, 54* and *55* in Portrush, the
last two again from the GN section. On 11 June *10* too had
another look at the North Atlantic and *4, 5, 6,* and *54* were
also there. It was certainly another great summer for the
excursionists. The small band of railwaymen who dealt with
this influx each Satuday doubtless enjoyed it, each in his
own way, from the jovial figure of the foreman, Bob Bowman
(page 106), to the pipe-smoking signalman, John Murdoch.
All those summer frocks and youthful limbs, shapely and
unshapely, may well have been the reason for Murdoch's
frequent use of binoculars from the cabin window, but loyal
colleagues always assured me that the primary interest was
in boating.

For its last summer timetable the UTA had the first deliveries
of their 'Hampshire' type diesel electric units. Their much
greater horsepower just about compensated for the more
numerous MED and MPD type units, out of service through
arrears of maintenance. Steam requirements were therefore

very much as for 1965, with Saturday mainline departures from Belfast at 5.55am, 8.35am and 8.50am, and rather more activity on the Larne line than in former years. By now news of the steam exploits of the previous year had filtered through even to folk who never give railways a thought except at the holiday season. 'Enthusiasts' who in ordinary circumstances would have been greatly exercised to distinguish one uniformed railwayman from another were now talking glibly of Alan Robinson etc and making a weekly visit to Portrush by rail a Saturday ritual.

If one regards as an era in itself the period from the arrival of MPD units on the NCC mainline until the commencement of the spoil project at the end of this year I think over this period *3* was the most reliably good engine on Portrush trains, even though *4, 7, 10* and *52* had their years of special glory. Tables C, J and N all demonstrate 1966 examples of this. What indeed can one say about another Alan Robinson run, that with *3* on the 7.30pm? Nuisance though it was, one cannot honestly blame the Aughleish gatekeeper, surprised at such a fast time from Ballymena, and anyway it was of little conse-quence, for 'Maggie' was making one of her legendary unsched-uled return trips from Ballymena hospital. The way this special stop at Cookstown Junction was arranged and accepted without question seemed obviously to derive from NCC-type humanity but I often pondered at some deeper significance.

With half as big a train again on 20 July one would not expect another run by *3* on the 7.30pm to compare for sect-ional times, but Harry Ramsey finished up in good style for this load with a time of 26min 14sec in from Antrim, 78mph at Greencastle providing for seaside trippers that special NCC thrill so near a city terminus. A week later the load was down to six bogies so that Paddy Shannon adjusted his running to the situation in his usual competent style to ensure that *4* should join the restricted ranks of engines which have brought the 7.30pm in before time.

There was at least variety in trying out the tanks based on

the Great Northern as they settled back in York Road. With *51* and eight bogies on the 2.10pm ex Derry, Crymble reached Belfast from Ballymena in a net 34min on 23 July, and 65mph with *53* on the 2.15pm ex Portrush with the same load was an agreeable sprint from Coulter, which included an unusual nonstop sectional time of 28min 40sec from Macfin to Cullybackey. The report about *50* was less cheerful, the mitigating excuse this time being the lack of a tablet catcher. This became an increasing handicap, though somewhat lessened by the reduction in block sections, for this was Glarryford's last summer as such.

Some readers, long since satiated with the never ending Portrush saga, may be glad to retreat, if only temporarily, to a different setting. To a NCC man *56* would have seemed far too good material to be abandoned to lifting train duties in the wilds of Pomeroy, but this was apparently how Adelaide saw her possibilities. Thus employed, on 17 July, *56* got out of control and incurred considerable damage. *51* had then to return to Adelaide to take her place, for *54* and *55* were in fairly frequent demand for specials to Dublin.

Without *51*, York Road found themselves short for the big Derry day on 13 August, so the only solution was to resurrect for one day *57*, which in May had made what looked like a last run when she hauled *7* to Ballymena, where both had lain since. It occurs to me here that these two engines and *54* almost certainly made their last recorded passenger runs on foreign (GNR) rails. If this seems a sombre finish for good NCC engines it should not be forgotten that more than half the moguls had the same experience.

I did not witness *57*'s shunting activities at York Road myself, having travelled to Derry with the first special at 7.10am. Tom Crymble had *6* for this ten bogie train and with five stops and various other delays it was reasonable work to be only 5min late on a 2hr 35min schedule. Another special from Belfast had *10*, those from Ballymena, Ballymoney and Coleraine being hauled by *53*, *4* and *9* respectively. *55* was borrowed from the GN for an Antrim special and *5* had the ordinary 8.50am. Finally *50* repeated the experience (though hardly the speed) of that July day seven years ago by working the 12.50pm through to Derry.

In early November Adelaide running shed was closed. Though little time was wasted in rendering unrecognisable the site of this once largest locomotive shed of the Great Northern, the demolition of the corresponding NCC one at York Road in 1971 was even more sudden and complete. When *54* had hauled *55* to York Road and *51*, hauling *56*, had made the same journey the following day, NCC steam relations with the GNR seemed to have come full circle.

40min nonstop was the best time, in post-war days, that the authorities would ever book for steam expresses to Ballymena, so anything substantially under this is always worth nothing, especially when it is made in mid-winter as late as 1966. Thinly disguised as parcels reliefs a few steam passenger workings reached Derry around the Christmas period. Table B shows *4* with the Courtaulds partnership of Crawley and Nicholl on one of these.

The Courtaulds contract had now been lost, presumably with a very light heart, as neither the engine position nor the availability of paths on the Larne line seemed geared to cope with both this and the spoil trains. As the first of the new hopper wagons began to arrive, they could be seen running in on ballast trains or with engine alone. Hearts were high at York Road. There was going to be plenty of work for every driver and fireman available. There would also be plenty of overtime and probably the railway too might make some money.

1967

Despite working the 5pm to Larne Harbour on 28 December *9* was withdrawn early in the New Year several months after *1*. A period in the works during 1966 had apparently been a sheer waste of time, and the management considered that

201

eleven engines were adequate for a heavy project likely to last over three years. As usual their serious thoughts were concerned with diesels, in this case the continuing crisis of the unreliability of the MED and MPD type units, which was to be remedied by yet another expensive re-engining. It seemed that the new diesel electric units could carry them through until this was done. Maybe the summer would be wet, with little extra traffic. If not then there were those steam engines.

In fact one of the most highly thought of engines, *54*, lasted only until March. Great Northern enginemen had been criticised when this engine had dropped her lead plugs on a couple of occasions but now it transpired that the fault was with the boiler shop at Swindon. She had run some 32,000 miles only with this new firebox but facilities at York Road for boiler work were now almost nil. So *54* was left to rot beside the running shed, a constant reminder of the realities of steam as NIR saw it.

It was unfortunate that *54*, although she did perform on the spoil trains for a few weeks, had not lasted till Easter for it seemed that all the worst engines were used on the Portrush specials. Nothing of any quality was reported about *4, 6, 50* or *51*. On 14 April the van at the rear of the 8.35am diesel ex Derry became badly derailed near Greencastle. This was a train often patronised by the UTA chairman, Sir Arthur Algeo, but he had other things on his mind at that time and on 8 May created a sensation in transport circles by dismissing the manager, John Coulthard, who 2½ years later was to receive over £6000 in settlement of a resulting court action. The rank and file railwayman tends to a cynical conviction that wholesale sacking of the executives would do no great harm. But Coulthard's attitude to the railway had already won him a few friends amongst the men so his dismissal was a sure sign to the rest of them that he had been the kind of 'boss' the railway needed and the news was followed by a two hour stoppage of work as a protest.

A suitable reaction came the following Saturday when the

9.35am Sunday School special from York Road touched 74mph at Dunadry with *10* piloted by *53*. The pilot came off at Ballymena to work forward to Derry a CIE goods with which NIR diesels had come to grief early that morning. *10* continued by herself, as she should have been throughout, of course, and fared badly, so the ready-made assistance had been lucky. This train was followed by a RPSI enthusiasts' special, hauled as far as Ballymena by *55*. Here their own engine, 0-6-0 *186*, came on as pilot to provide, in good weather, photographic interest by frolicking up and down the Portrush branch. In the evening *53* turned up again to pilot *55* home from Ballymena, so it had certainly been a day for double headed trains, three variations being noted.

By 3 June the Saturday-Sunday school season was in full spate, providing a steam run to Portrush for the more robust. One could have endured outpourings of youthful exuberance, such as incessant running up and down the carriages, the water pistols and the bubble gum, with more fortitude if there had been any great possibility of good running. In pleasant travelling conditions the manner in which these very heavy trains recovered from slowings for tablet exchange could have had its attraction. One rather better experience was on 24 June when *4, 51, 53* and *55* were all in Portrush. With a big train of 330 tons to form the 6.55pm special *4* ran nonstop from Ballyboyland loop to Belfast in 63min for the 47¾ miles. One should not judge such a run purely on an average speed basis, though on the GNR 70min for 50¾ miles to Warrenpoint was considered exceptionally fast. Rather, tablet slows at Dunloy and Cullybackey, the restriction through Ballymena and a pw slowing at Ballyclare Junction should all be taken into account as well as a slow finish, for the schedule gave them 65min. Inspector Dunlop and Crymble were probably sharing the driving on this occasion and also giving assistance to the fireman, Willie Graham. A passing time of 11¾min Ballymena–Antrim was, in fact, even time.

Throughout the summer *51* seemed by sheer willingness rather than brilliance to be the most useful engine at York

Road. However, on 3 July with a Coleraine driver in some
trouble this engine took no less than 23½min Whiteabbey-
Mossley, pass to pass, which is rather a long time to be
averaging 10mph, even with ten bogies. This was a special to
Derry, but with the same set of carriages and the same engine
the very next day Joe Cairns had no trouble in running from
Portrush to Ballymoney in 25min 53sec, allowed 27. This
was a Sunday School excursion, but the shorter distance
from Ballymoney to Portrush by road is probably only one
reason why specials specifically for this station have been
rare in modern times. This contrasts greatly, for instance, with
Bank Holiday Monday, 1936, when, in addition to a generous
service of through trains, specials left Ballymoney at 11.5am,
11.25am, 1.10pm, 2.20pm, 6.55pm, 10.55pm and 11.25pm,
the last two being empties, of course, returning to Coleraine.

On 5 July, it seemed that another count of resources had
been taken with unsatisfactory results, for *10* hauled *48* (both
engines in steam) from Adelaide to York Road. The Great
Northern 0-6-0 shunted for a few days, even visiting the
docks, but was soon condemned and withdrawn. The following week *56* was put into the works to have damaged parts
replaced by the pony truck and smokebox door off withdrawn *9*. One was inclined to wonder why this obvious move
had been delayed so long.

The upsurge in Derry traffic seen after the Great Northern
closure had quickly abated and although the 8.50am to Derry
no longer ran the 8.35am was sometimes down to six bogies
this summer, a sad falling off. Table C shows what a sporting
young crew could achieve with *51* on this train. The combined
ages of Jack Kitchen and Willie Graham can have been little in
excess of forty, at which many men were still firing before
World War II.

The threadbare condition of her driving wheel tyres was
only one reminder that *3* was now 3½ years since last overhaul, but Dan McAtamney's run in Table B gave no hint of
this run-down, the speed through Cookstown Junction being
a special feature of this superb example of sustained express

travel. There was always a special thrill about twisting through here at over 60mph but a recent development has been to remove the old island platform and straighten out the track. Rather ironically there is now an overall speed restriction of 60mph, not existing at the time of Dan's run. Steam appeared quite frequently on the 1.15pm to Portrush this summer and during John Moore's week early in August he had *3* on one occasion, getting away to 74mph at Templepatrick, only to be checked at Kilmakee gates.

55 tended to be as unreliable as *3* was consistent and on 15 July *55* sustained a broken bogie spring with McAtamney, coming down with an 8.45 special to Portrush. Pathetically feeble were the facilities now available for repair at Coleraine, so *55* set off light for Belfast. Held at Dunloy to let *51* through with the 12.45 ex Derry, *55* was next despatched back down the line to assist the diesel 14.05 ex Portrush (NIR was now converted to the 24 hour system). Some time later a number of amateur photographers at Ballymena felt they had the scoop of the year when *55* arrived, broken spring and all, hauling that 14.05, the first vehicle of which was MPD unit *55*. In contrast, Table N shows *55* behaving in exemplary fashion, and later in the run Sloane had her up to 61mph *before* Macfin. 72mph at Kellswater was also of at least North Atlantic Express class but throughout this run gatekeepers' work and the operating were both at a low ebb, rendering almost negative all this effort.

55 had also been in Derry on 12 July, when *4* and *51* also worked Orangemen's specials, but it was *3* which established herself in Derry this year for the Bank Holiday week's specials to Portrush. As was the usual custom she then remained till 12 August to work a big train of empty carriages from Derry to Coleraine, returning with that area's selection of Apprentice Boys. Other specials arriving in Derry were from Ballymena (*53*), Antrim (*10*) and Belfast (*56* and *55*). The ordinary 8.35 to Derry was strengthened and worked by *4* at an altered time of 9am. Later the mystery engine *5* arrived with the 13.00 ex Belfast and was a very surprising choice to head the procession of return traffic, *53* being the engine sent home early on the 12.45. The whole affair reflected considerable credit on the loco inspector on a day when the rain seldom let up and Coleraine provided a points failure for return traffic.

There was one obvious omission from these specials, the engine most recently outshopped, *6*. During this period her only passenger work was an occasional Larne train, and this only because the better engines were constantly employed with the spoil traffic. It was now more or less a one-man band which was responsible for a day to day maintenance of the steam engines and a pretty thankless job Rab McDonald had of it. Here was a tradition of steam, for his father and uncle had both been drivers.

Most evenings day trippers at Portrush returned to Ballymena and Belfast on the 19.30, invariably with a good sprinkling of steam enthusiasts, to enjoy the noise and general atmosphere of effort required for a heavy train rather than any possibility of high speed. For the space available here it is impossible and possibly unneccessary to remind them in detail of this aspect of the tanks' Indian summer but the following summary of my own 19.30 experiences may serve some purpose.

	2-6-4T No	driver	fireman	bogies	
8 July	*51*	F. Dunlop	J.D. Kitchen	7	3½ late
13 July	*55*	D. McDonald	B. Nicholl	9	37 late
15 July	*53*	P. Shannon	B. McCrory	8	33 late
18 July	*51*	T. Crymble	D. Kernoghan	10	21½ late
17 July	*51*	J.D. Kitchen	G. Robinson	8	8 late
19 July	*51*	T. Crymble	T. Dean	7	TIME
20 July	*51*	T. Crymble	G. Robinson	8	½ late
22 July	*4*	W.J. McConnell		7	6 late
5 August	*51*	J. Simpson	R. Robinson	10	28 late
8 August	*53*	S. Sloane		5	2 late
9 August	*53*	S. Sloane		5	½ late
2 September	*5*	P. Shannon	G. Phelan	7	14 late

The punctuality aspect is not always an accurate guide to

the interest or quality of the run, of course. Most of these trains were packed with passengers, and many holiday visitors to Portrush, possibly with little better to do, seemed to make it a ritual to witness the departure, some even making the run as far as Coleraine so that small children might have their first and possibly their last experience of a mainline steam train.

The schedule of 1¾ hours with six stops was probably beyond the ability of any diesel except the new Hampshire type, if trailers were attached, but a well handled tank could still keep time, even with hand tablet exchange, unless the load exceeded eight bogies. The allowance on the first section had been increased to 15min, possibly because of a 15mph restriction on a bridge just outside Portrush. This could easily be cut despite inevitable signal checks approaching Coleraine. On 19 July times with *51* of 11min 16sec to Coleraine and 12min 18sec to Ballymoney were particularly good but the best actual speed before Coleraine with the 19.30 this summer was with *4* by W.J. McConnell of Tamlaght, and Coleraine shed. Reputed to have a healthy distrust of the true purpose of distant signals McConnell showed no undue concern about the mechanical condition of *4*, by now fast deteriorating. In fact he had been expecting to drive a diesel and, having lost his cap, then disappeared into the shopping area of Portrush to return resplendent in a gay check.

None of this year's runs on the 19.30 justify inclusion in the log tables, the dominating feature being really *51*'s ability to keep going. It looked as if it was her mogul boiler which put her in a different class from the others for heavy slogging. *98* had been a great old horse for the long drag and one did sense that it was her boiler which was now sustaining *51*, but of all the moguls I think it was *101* which *51*, no greyhound at the best of times, resembled during this, her most· outstanding year. It would have been interesting to have had one or other of the two drivers (McAtamney and McDonald) who had her so long on spoil duties, for a 19.30 run with her. Towards the end, the latter driver used to produce astronomical figures in an effort to indicate the mileage she must have reached by now and certainly, of all ten engines *51* was the one most often used for the spoil traffic. Even in 1967 *51*'s mileage of 31,747 was only 29 miles less than the most used engine (but less on spoil trains), *4*. These totals indicate how much more active York Road tanks had become since 1965.

On 4 September Monkstown halt was re-opened but even the modest service offered was soon reduced and I should imagine that any revenue which resulted from this enterprise would scarcely have paid for the repainting of the halt's nameboard. Possibly persisting with a more frequent service might have in the end been fruitful but in fact the halt was now badly sited for serving new estates.

Further RPSI railtours brought *186* again onto the main line on 9 September (for Dundalk) and on 28 October, when the last Irish 0-6-4 tank, *27*, also sampled Dunadry bank. The new civil engineer, R.P. Beattie, made a trip to Derry on 15 November, presumably for inspection purposes, and *4* was used to propel Saloon 150, in dark blue livery (former GNR 50 of the 1953 royal train).

1968

During the first two months of this year, when *5, 6, 50, 51, 55* and *56* were frequently employed on the spoil trains, two new aspects of track repair operations became evident. It was at least twenty years since there had been so much of this kind of activity and on Sundays, when the spoil wagons were normally out of use, they were now frequently used for discharging stone ballast, something for which they were not entirely suited, of course, but NIR stock of ordinary ballast wagons was now nearly as low as their few brakevans, this railway going in for more elaborate embellishments, such as expensive tamping machines. On Sundays also, as well as at least twice during each week, ballast trains ran from Antrim (where the stone was unloaded from lorries) to various parts of the GNR main line, a frequent incursion by the tank engines into non-steam territory which no one had expected

to see again. Except on a very occasional Sunday, *3* completely dominated these workings, as she was considered the worst
engine, though she certainly did not sound so. Great Northern
crews were responsible for this working, even the York Road–
Antrim section, so that a typical NCC comment was that if *3*
wasn't too bad now she soon would be.

On 27 March yet another RPSI railtour provided *27* on the
Larne line, this time, and then the little Guinness tank on a
splendidly conceived tour of Belfast docks. Much of this day
was extremely wet and it must be admitted that 'Midland'
regional manager (yes! NIR was now divided into regions)
T.N. Topley and various harbour police and bystanders did
well to keep a straight face as the cortège of 'flats' passed
along at a dignified gait, loaded up with some very wet
enthusiasts.

Although I have tried to provide variety of both engines
and men in the log tables, Table B is exceptional in that one
driver's name appears three times. I have already mentioned
McAtamney's run with *3* and now on Easter Saturday, 1968,
was an occasion properly recorded when the best ever 35
minute timing of the North Atlantic express was bettered.
True, the load was light, even lighter than was normal on that
5.15pm of pre-war days, but *53* was well ahead of *93* (in the
same table) all the way and, in fact, if Dan had run from
Doagh forward, as his run with *3* shows he well could, a
quite remarkable time of 32½min to Ballymena could have
resulted to make a little less unlikely all the tall stories about
half hour runs. It was indeed satisfactory that some winter
attention in the shops had so transformed *53* from the ill-
sounding engine of the previous summer.

An engine which had done even less of note during 1967
than *53* was *56* and the very same day she produced another
statistical improvement, though less momentous, when
Dobbin ran well to pass milepost 52 from a stop at Dunloy in
7min 21sec. This was with a 15.00 relief to Portrush. Yet
another record of its kind occurred on Easter Monday when a
double-headed 9.25, loaded to nine bogies, fractionally

exceeded 80mph at Dunadry. The same engines and drivers normally worked at each end of a spoil train, at little more than a quarter of this speed. The pilot engine was *50* with Alan Robinson, *55* with Tom Crymble continuing forward from Antrim unaided, losing some time. This had been an unexpected and quite remarkable variation of their daily chore and 23min 45sec with this load had been a fine time to Antrim.

The return Portrush traffic on the two holiday evenings had nothing in the way of good running worth mentioning because *50*, yet again, was in rebellious mood, nor was *51* any better. With the 19.30 on Tuesday night Ballymena was left 17 minutes late by *50* with nine bogies. At Kingsbog we ground to an unexpected stop because the police desired to search the train. It was impossible to gather from their type of questioning exactly what their problem was but driver Rob Graham came along to inform me that a complaint had been made by some female at Ballymena about an attempt at rape, experienced during the journey from Portrush. Past observation of the mêlée and general pandemonium of a typical Easter Tuesday return excursion would not have led me to expect any kind of reluctant attitude from most of the fair sex on view. However, it seems that someone was eventually charged with a form of assault.

It was now like old times to observe NCC engines with the same crews every day, as had the regular spoil engines, *50* and *55* on one train and *51* and *56* on the other. Robinson and Graham had *50* with Crymble and Mitchell on *55*. On the other train McAtamney and McGarvey had *51*, and *56* was driven by R.J. Simpson and T.H. Ramsey. Later retirements and resignations in the senior (diesel) link saw the departures of Nelson, Lamont, Moore, Sloane and Shannon which provided *50, 51* and *55* with new drivers in the form of Dobbin and McAlees, McDonald and Kitchen, and Wright and Gillespie. This left *56* the only engine to retain the same crews throughout but the engine herself did not last the pace, unfortunately.

On 1 June the atmosphere at Whiteabbey seemed timeless as a tea urn and many crates of lemonade were parked at the end of a platform gay with a variety of summer frocks. This 9.35 excursion ex Belfast arrived with *50* and one of her regular drivers Graham had no trouble getting a train of at least 330 tons away and up the 1/76. A new obstacle for Portrush trains from about this time was the 'two mile' bridge, just that distance south of Coleraine. The straightening and widening of the road here virtually turned bridge 179 into a tunnel, a 10mph slack being imposed on all trains, until it was completed in 1969.

If anything, the traffic was even heavier this year and the steam engines performed really noble work in coping with it. In one week I travelled on the 13.15 to Portrush five times, with a nice variety (for 1968) of *10, 6* (twice) and *53* (twice). The driver on four of the occasions was the only ex-BCDR man left on the NCC, Willie Lamont, a good engineman and decent mate on the footplate but unlikely to provide even the most mild kind of thrill for the speed-lover.

The carriages for this train returned on the 19.30, though normally, of course, much more fully loaded. Again a few lines in statistical form seems the best way to summarise, for 1968, this 19.30.

	2-6-4T	driver	fireman	bogies	
13 July	*53*	P. McCann	R. Robinson	7	38 late (Ballymena)
15 July	*53*	W. McAlees	J. Magill	10	17 late (Whiteabbey)
16 July	*6*	P. Mitchell	A. McMenamin	10	30 late
17 July	*6*	P. Mitchell	A. McMenamin	10	20 late (Whiteabbey)
18 July	*10*	J. Simpson	W. Graham	10	46½ late
19 July	*53*	R.J. Simpson	T. McCrum	8	16 late (Whiteabbey)
20 July	*53*	W. Lamont (F. Dunlop)	T. McCrum	9	8 late
27 July	*51*	G. Houston	R. Robinson	10	42 late
3 August	*51*	T. Dean	T. McCrum	7	1 early

The closure of Macfin cabin the previous November and the extension of the Electric Direction Control Lever system to Ballymoney should have improved punctuality this summer but naturally the slack at bridge 179 did not help. However, most of the lateness was due to the amazing optimism of the planners, who just ignored the clear evidence of 1967 operation of this train. As they saw it the diesel set of the 13.15 would complete several local trips between Portrush and Coleraine with the connection of the 17.45 ex Belfast at 19.03 ex Coleraine, and then the 19.30 Portrush-Belfast. When this 13.15 was diesel the arrangement only worked successfully if the 17.45 ran to time, which was seldom. When the 13.15 was steam her crew had to plan shunting and watering with care, even if the 17.45 was on time, for a punctual exit from Portrush to be even a remote possibility. If R.J. Simpson was in good humour this was just the situation for him and on 19 July, with two bogies, he reduced the 15min schedule to Portrush of the 19.03 to a mere 9min 37sec, surely a record low percentage of time allowed. Even after this energy, however, departure from Portrush was 12min late. The previous night it had been 21min late.

This struggle home in the evening from Portrush with heavy trains, a feature of this railway since pre-mogul days, depended more on good steaming than fast running, so a new speed restriction of 60mph, introduced on 17 July, affected the 19.30 less than most. With no speedometer anyhow, the NCC steam driver had always depended upon his own judgement. The 19.30 was booked nonstop from Antrim to Belfast, of course, Whiteabbey's encroachment in the summary being due to guard Tom Simpson, anxious that Larne line passengers (like myself) could thus catch the 21.20 ex York Road there, when running late.

Another new feature of 1968 was the construction and opening, on 12 June, of University Halt, less than a mile from Coleraine on the Portrush branch. An interesting train, as a result, was the 17.35 ex Coleraine, which ran just to University and back. On the few occasions when all they had was a

tank engine to work it, the train was propelled from the
Coleraine direction and on 17 July, for instance, with two
bogies and *53*, R.J. Simpson was back again into Coleraine
6½min after first leaving, possibly some kind of record for an
Irish steam train. Thus, instead of being closed for most of the
year while Portrush council worried and argued about possible
complete closure, the branch began to have a frequent service
quite well supported by the graduates in particular, and open
all the year round.

On 8 July *10* was doing the ballast run to the Great
Northern and *5* had a train of bad order wagons from Coleraine. Some were already smoking and had to be taken off at
Ballymena. While Speers Wiseman, the foreman there, was
engaged in badinage with the signalman and guard I heard
someone inquire of the driver, Davie McDonald, the reason
for the train. The answer given was pure NCC humour, perfectly expressed in this big, often dour, man. Without a smile
McDonald replied that the wagons were required for the
Orangemen next week.

Needless to say, when I went to Limavady Junction on 12
July to intercept two specials from Derry I wasn't expecting
to see any wagons loaded up with Orangemen and didn't. The
first I photographed at Myroe crossing, and on my way there
met a flute band led by a gorgeously dressed individual who
hailed me enthusiastically as they passed. Later, as they
boarded the second special I had the opportunity to study
him more carefully and soon identified him as Willie John
Keilly, signalman at Ballykelly Airfield cabin (closed July
1971). The first special had been headed by *50*, already in
trouble with a hot big end. *56* with her usual crew of R.J.
Simpson and Albert Plews, had ten bogies on the second and
reached Coleraine in 27min, the booked stop at Castlerock
not being made. This deviation from the printed instructions
was a typical piece of NCC extemporisation, which has left
many an enterprising enthusiast stranded.

Traditionally the following day, 13 July, usually left
'demonstration' traffic to the Great Northern, preoccupied

with the 'sham fight' at Scarva. To everyone's surprise, *55* was sent over to assist with the traffic, thus providing steam passenger trains on the GN section in 1968, whereas 1967 had been a completely blank year. On this date also, for the second successive year, McAtamney made a fine run to Ballymena. *6*'s fireman on this occasion (Table B) was Tom McCrum.

A special which had become traditional since the closure of the GN Derry line had its return working this year on 25 July. Almost certainly the only non-Irish-speaking passenger in the packed ten bogie train run for students returning from Donegal, I noted that the railway evidently thought this 14.25 special important enough to have Inspector Frank Dunlop up on the engine and Chief Inspector Sam Hanley in the train. A timing of 142min to Belfast with this load was not too sluggish and there was no mistaking the pride in Hanley's voice as he drew my attention to an arrival at platform 4 one minute before time. Gillespie drove *53* very sensibly, with nothing faster than 65mph (before braking for Monkstown) after three intermediate stops and three other slowings.

As a contrast, suitably mentioned at this point, was a special to Derry redolent of another kind of 'culture', on 9 November, for which Alan Robinson had his regular engine, *50*. This was organised by the Rev. Ian Paisley for 'Loyalist' supporters and it was stopped at Ballymena for examination because of a bomb scare. 'There's damn all bomb,' Inspector Hanley was overheard to say, and so indeed it proved after a stop of 9 minutes. A month later the same cleric organised further specials, to Larne Harbour, to greet a former gun-running ship of historic interest. In fact only one (worked by *55*) was justified but vociferous instructions about clean engines were conveyed to York Road shed, which presumably did no harm to steam morale.

Previously, the yearly visit of the Apprentice Boys to Derry on 10 August had provided the last occasion when more than two steam engines were at Waterside on the same day. Here for the last time were the merits of the top engines suggested by the trains they were chosen to work. The 7.20 and 7.45 specials ex Belfast were in charge of *4* and *56*. The engines for the 9.05 Ballymena special (*50*) and the 9.12 Antrim special (*51*) each piloted one of the first two specials out of Belfast. *10* worked the 10.14 special ex Coleraine and, as usual, the proceedings closed with the ordinary 8.35 (altered to 9.00), which included, traditionally, saloon 162 (still provided on Linfield specials for their directors, so it had the correct aroma) hauled by *53. 56* was unfit to return in the evening so *3* was lit up for the 18.25 special. It was apt that this latter engine, better known around Derry than any other tank except *55*, should take a share on such an occasion. By the following spring, both *3* and *56* would have had their last failure of all, to make certain that 10 August 1968 should be their last Protestant demonstration.

This event always quickly followed Derry holiday week and this year that city was just in the early stages of the most modern proof of the aptness of Dr Johnson's famous adage about patriotism. The planners on the railway had been stating confidently that the new diesels, easily capable of hauling nine steam carriages on the level, could handle all the traffic themselves, so it was a pleasant surprise to find steam quite active after all. Table N shows the heaviest of the specials I experienced and it was interesting that after taking no part in passenger work all summer *51* was sent to Derry for this, on the Monday, still a Bank Holiday in the Republic of Ireland, adjacent to Derry. The uninhibited McConnell had *10* on the afternoon excursion on two occasions during this week and I regret not having the space to include in the tables his run on the 14.05 special on 9 August, by which time the load was down to six bogies. This was a typical express load of former days and Willie John's time to Coleraine of 46¾min with three intermediate stops was quite up to express running in best steam days. It was good to see *10* run as freely as ever, reaching at least 60mph on each section.

The most exciting of many good runs in 1,968 was on 6 July and appears in Table A. Manned by McDonald and

McCrum, *53* had come down to York Road station from the shed for a special, but it was found possible to pack the parties concerned into a diesel so *53* was held for the 10.50 ordinary passenger to Portrush, for which this diesel had been booked. While the engine's crew was waiting for these decisions to be made, one of the management, not noted for interesting himself in the engines from one year to the next, pompously inquired of McDonald why his engine was being allowed to blow off steam. As I am not a lip-reader I cannot confirm the exact vocabulary used in what was clearly an extremely concise reply. Possibly this slur on his enginemanship penetrated beneath Davie's normally fairly conservative approach to driving. I cannot otherwise quite account for the exceptional quality of *53*'s descent of Dunadry bank, almost certainly the fastest recorded run by an Irish steam engine since 1953. That very afternoon Kitchen and Plews extracted yet another fine run from *4*, as shown in Table D, and a week later a shining *56* was also competing with pre-war statistics. Table I shows the essential features of Simpson's running but can give no idea of the look of alarm on signalman Charlie Knox's face at Ballyboyland when he saw a train approach at nearly 50mph, with obviously no intention of braking for the tablet exchange.

Yet another run by *4* had in quality neither the fiery temperament of 'Batman' Simpson, the disgusted disillusion of McDonald nor the youthful exuberance of Kitchen. Table K shows how Crymble, clearly determined at first to run exactly to time without any histrionics, was forced by a bad signal check to extract from his regular fireman Arthur McMenamin enough steam for this remarkable climb.

53 should also get another mention if only to acknowledge some enterprising driving from a man reared on the Great Northern. Having gradually dispersed the large number of enginemen redundant from the BCDR, the NCC had now two former Portadown men on their books, Jimmy Donnelly and Peter McCann. The latter driver had the 15.05 to Portrush on 13 July and showed the utmost confidence in handling eight

bogies. Doubtless a spell of firing on the tanks over the bank
to Dundalk had given useful experience, but the manner in
which he raced away from the summit to 74mph after
Ballymartin gates showed a very different approach from
standard GNR practice before Bessbrook, coming north,
in modern times.

The winter timetable still showed catering facilities on each
of the four main Derry–Belfast trains and indeed, in somewhat erratic fashion, this has persisted up to the present time.
The 1968 standard can best be judged by a journey I had
home from Derry, where I was probably at fault in preferring
a 'steam' coach at the rear, from which there was no access
through the DE power unit into the main part of the train
where the refreshment car was. It was Ballymena before I
reached this vehicle but the chap in charge of this Belfast-
based car insisted that tea 'was finished'. So I produced a
timetable which indicated refreshment facilities, whereupon
the change in his attitude was quite remarkable, for not only
did he make me a fresh cup of tea immediately, but the
charge was less than normally made by the deft-footed individual in the Derry-based car.

I mention this as just one aspect of a policy whereby
accepted railway facilities, such as toilets on trains (and even
in stations), waiting rooms and even platform seats, were
gradually being withdrawn. Though a cup of tea could now
apparently represent a problem for a train advertising 'light
refreshments', as recently as 1966 breakfast had been served
on the 8.30am ex Derry and à la carte meals on the other
three. This could hardly have anything to do with the fact
that Sir Arthur Algeo had lived in Ballymoney and his successor in Belfast. A couple of years previously traditional NCC
enterprise had still been offering snacks such as egg and chips
on its Derry trains. In 1955 it had been possible to get lunch
and even dinner for as little as 5s 6d and a good high tea for
4s 6d. Three trains in each direction between Derry and
Belfast had dining facilities, this being doubled in the summer
on Saturdays. A dining car on the 2.40pm to Portrush on

217

Fridays was a variation intolerable to the modern type of management. Comparing all this with pre-war conditions, the four trains to Derry had then all tea cars, as had the 12 noon to Portrush. More famous, of course, was the buffet car to Portrush on the North Atlantic Express and the Golfers' Express had a dining car and a saloon.

1969

Early in this year there was a strike at the spoil sidings of short duration. In this case the railwaymen were not the cause of the period of inactivity but it may have given them food for thought when one considers the number of one-day and longer stoppages inflicted on the public later this year and the following year.

Easter produced such dominance by steam at Portrush that it gave many of us more confidence about the future than we had felt ten years before. Logically this was probably wrong and so indeed, within less than six months, it was to prove. The ex GNR 4-4-0 *171* was still the property of NIR but the RPSI, which rented her services on a yearly basis, had managed to finance a very expensive overhaul at Harland & Wolff's during the winter, so an attractive arrangement was made whereby she would work on an Easter Tuesday excursion train to Portrush. Before this she had, of course, to be run in, and a nostalgic job in this respect was performed on 3 April when the steam crane was worked to Knockmore Junction in connection with a derailment of the CIE Derry goods. The driver in charge of the diesel-hauled goods on this occasion was the same who, many years before, had completely destroyed a single line tablet by throwing it, with the remains of his lunch, into an engine's firebox.

In ordinary circumstances the ballast engine *3* would probably have had this job with the crane, but on 19 March she had lost a slidebar with a ballast train near Bellarena, being hauled up for her last mainline journey, prior to complete withdrawal, by *55*. My journeys home from Portrush on Easter Monday and Tuesday both had an element of interest.

218

The run with *56* on the Monday with a crew of Paddy Dobbin and Davie Smith (son of 'Gunboat') was to prove to be my last with this engine, for she smashed a cylinder three weeks later at Magheramorne. *3* and *54* were both tried for replacements, without success or indeed much enthusiasm. It was rather like *54*'s withdrawal all over again, for there was no drive from the top to keep a good engine in service. £1000 for scrap was, it seemed, a much more vital figure than another 50,000 miles of heavy haulage and *56*'s new firebox had been involved in only 80,000 miles to date, only a fifth of the NCC standard. Her total mileage run was just over 8000 less than *54*'s and nearly 174,000 less than *3*'s which had run 709,441 miles.

The final run up from Portrush with *56* had been fraught with delays but it is pleasant to record that with the nine bogies 60mph was exceeded after Glarryford, Cookstown Junction and Mossley, which was certainly not always the case. The run up the following day, with the same driver, is given in Table K as the last time I was to reach Belfast from Ballymena in under 35min. *171*'s tryout, with a modest seven bogie train, was far from exciting and by Portrush she had developed a hot big end. So at Coleraine all hands were enlisted to shovel her coal into *53*'s bunker while *10* came light from Belfast to fill the gap. The previous day this engine had also come down from Belfast in an emergency, when it was decided that resources could not cope with all the return traffic and *4* was sent to Antrim for the last set of carriages.

Once engines began to appear on the GN ballast (to replace *3*) their passenger work was usually as good as over and *10* had been an unexpected arrival at Portrush at Easter. She could now lay claim to be the filthiest, most battered looking engine ever to claim NCC kinship. Footplate travel, too, though still more smooth than a mogul's, was unbelievably noisy for this class. For some time, broken engine springs had been a repeated cause of upsets in the spoil schedule so early in the year the most active engines benefitted from an addition to the dwindling stocks. *50*, a regular offender though probably the most smooth running engine, received new springs together with *4, 53* and *51*, the latter now with seriously threadworn tyres. *55* was not included and for a time was little used, though still retaining the useful extended bunker from her days on the Dublin trains. *54*'s extension had been fitted to *56* and to enable coal to last an engine all day *4, 50, 51* and *53* had all now the extended bunker.

Two specials went to Portrush on 24 May, *4* hauling the 9.45 and *51* the 9.05, her first mainline passenger for over six months. The carriages involved in these two trains represented more than half the entire NIR steam stock, so a reference in detail here may help to give a picture of the last carriages running on the NCC. Of the twenty required that day seven were of GNR breed: two side corridor steels, one vestibule steel, two vestibule wooden coaches (one of which, 376, had figured in the last [as advertised] steam train to Dublin), a side corridor wooden coach, 386, and 236 (formerly GNR 415, a slip coach for use on the far off Oldcastle branch). The thirteen NCC carriages were of no less than seven different classes. The only surviving representatives of the famous North Atlantic quintet, 91-93, were there, renumbered 472, 240 and 392 respectively. There were also seven of the not greatly loved J6 and J12 side corridor seconds, dating back to the twenties, and two of the F3 class, once 1/2 compos. Finally there was 248, formerly 35, one of the tri-compo brakes, almost an inevitable class in an NCC set in steam days. The compartment type Larne 'steelers' could still at that time be seen decaying in Antrim goods yard.

The last day in May can be regarded as the grand slam of steam in Ireland because for the last time Antrim had six steam engines in one day and all on passenger trains. For the first time for some years a Portadown–Portrush through excursion was operated by steam, though only one of the complications now was that, as all engines were now at York Road, the mileage involved if one engine handled the train throughout was quite beyond the coal capacity of even the extended tank bunker. So *51, 6* and *10* were all involved in

the working of this one train, the latter engine having her
first recorded passenger run on the GN main line and very
bad it was too. The other engines active that day were *4* and
53 on Sunday School excursions to Portrush and *171* on a
RPSI trip to Coleraine which finished up at Great Victoria
Street.

It was rather typical of the authorities that, having put
their faith in diesel power since 1958, they should, eleven
years later, expect steam engines to haul, entirely unaided,
eleven bogies to Portrush, something very rarely resorted to
in steam days. However, in that era timekeeping was still a
matter of pride on the NCC. Now it was simply a case of
getting there sometime, somehow. It was quite a miracle
indeed, how it was managed to produce eleven carriages on
14 June for the 9.05 special when there were two more steam
specials to follow. Almost as remarkable was *53*'s achievement
in reaching Ballymena with this load in 49min 26sec. Inspector Dunlop was on the footplate with driver R.J. Simpson and
fireman Gaw and made no reference to the fact that Belfast
Inspector McCombe had given them this size of train, with no
assistance. So it was apparently some time after the summit
(minimum 12mph) that the crew realised what *53* had done.
Very impressive later was to get away to 58mph before Dunloy, and a start to stop time of 12min 12 sec from Coleraine
to Portrush (reached 2min early) was also excellent work.

On the same day Harry Ramsey and regular fireman Roy
Robinson, who usually had *53* on the spoil trains since the
demise of *56*, made a good run with *50* on a return Sunday
School excursion for the combined churches of the Ballyclare
and Doagh district, using the latter derelict station. This traditional excursion had ten bogies and was greeted at Doagh by
no less than the regional manager himself, who was no doubt
satisfied at an arrival so near to the time that the various
double-deck buses for the final part of the day were not being
delayed. Shortly after 10pm *5* could be heard battling across
Bleach Green viaduct with empty carriages destined for
Antrim, now the regular stabling point for steam carriages

since motorway requirements were gradually reducing siding space at York Road. On 28 June two return excursions from Portrush each had eleven bogies, the engines this time being *51* and *55*.

Portrush's last steam July arrived with nothing at all in the mainline timetable planned for steam, not even the last train home from Portrush each evening, now altered to 19.55, despite the lessons of the two previous years. This later departure was because the 17.45 ex York Road now left at 18.00, the Portrush connection now leaving Coleraine at 19.25. However, in yet another summer, steam had to be run on the 13.15 no less than ten times in July and once in August.

On most occasions Graham was the driver, working both his own week on the 13.15 and that of another driver, less enamoured with steam (page 106). Rob's competence and efficiency in 1969 conditions and the fact that *50* worked the train on every occasion but four resulted in a certain amount of predictability in the running, but relieved by a remarkable piece of skilful tablet exchange at Dunloy, a speed through of 60mph being eventually established as possibly another record. Despite frequent overtime at Cullybackey, waiting to cross a tardy diesel, and then a rather optimistic 20min timing to Ballymoney, arrivals at Portrush were reasonably punctual even though the big fore-man at Coleraine, Ernie Sinclair, might insert an additional stop for them at the new halt, Dhu Varren, in the manner of a local train. On 17 July, for instance, a nine bogie train could have been observed, only 3min late, making the short run from the halt into Portrush, and four days later this stop was again made but Portrush was reached on time.

Driving *50* on the spoil trains had helped Graham to esti-mate just how much punishment this engine would take, but on some of the evenings a driver not so familiar with her, such as Tom Smith of Ballymena, ran into trouble when, with a heavy train, he made a commendable attempt to work *50* a bit harder. On days when she was out of steam to have attention to her tubes, her substitute, *53* steamed better but was now greatly inferior in power, and on 24 July *55* had to be sent from Belfast to assist *53* from Antrim to Belfast, driver Gillespie. Table J details an interesting occasion when *50* worked home on the earlier 17.50 ex Portrush instead, the performance being better than was usually produced by the rostered MPD set.

The story of this time-honoured train ended (for steam) on 4 August with *53* in charge of Percy Mitchell and Davie Smith. 63mph before Dunminning (something we hadn't seen all summer) was cheerful but a late start resulted in arrival at Belfast 18min late. One final NIR train was worked into Portrush on 21 August when a through excursion from Larne for ICI workers had *6* into Belfast, *53* to Portrush and back and then *4* for the final stage for a train which reached Belfast from Portrush 76min late. Barney McCrory on *4* was a new driver for me and if he had not the fine black beard of *53*'s fireman, Gerry Phelan, his Victorian whiskers were impressive, nevertheless. Enginemen had not looked like this for nearly half a century. Barney ran out to Whiteabbey in good style in an attempt to recover some time but many of the excursion-ists were by now more than a little tipsy and on Whiteabbey platform had an angry argument with the guard about the train's lateness. A slight movement by the engine caused several more to fall onto the platform and the next day the guard was reported to the railway authorities by the excursion's organisers, who probably still had some very sore heads. A few weeks later this guard was discharged, though not apparently, for any proven misdemeanour on this occasion.

On 12 August steam had made its final contribution towards the Apprentice Boys by working two specials from Belfast to Derry, all others being diesel. T.H. Ramsey had *4* for the first special and about a section behind came *55*, driven by Davie McDonald. As we arrived at Waterside I thought it most apt that this engine, so long shedded at Derry should be in at the death. This was a day of disorder in a very troubled period in Derry's history but the most troubled sight to impress me during a fairly short stay was McDonald's face. The sight of a roofless shed, each engine as it was broken up, and every 'last' train seemed to affect him like a mortal blow. If for me an NCC engine is epitomised in the mogul type, both tank and tender, its human element is in the name McDonald, both Billy and Davie, for though not in any way related they were, in their different generations, veritable NCC barometers by reason of their sensitivity to both humour and pathos.

On 24 August bridge 219 at Lock crossing was being renewed. *51* went there overnight with a ballast train while *53* followed with the steam crane. I came upon the latter engine at Limavady Junction on her way home. Gillespie had decided that he had not enough water to make the next surviving column at Castlerock. An attempt then to use a hose, attached to a water tap, seemed to symbolise the end of NCC steam and in fact the last mainline passenger train for NIR requirements came a fortnight later, when *50* worked a football special to Ballymena on 6 September.

Epilogue

With the arrival of 1970 only seven NCC engines remained in service. Of these *55* was the only remnant of the exhaust injector quartet, *50* and *51* represented those with mogul boilers, *4* and *6* the last two to have heavy overhaul, *5* the first of the class and the most favoured by the boiler inspector, and finally *53*.

It seemed rather a depraved kind of occupation speculating which might go next, and unrewarding, for it was *50*, an extremely rare bird on the GN ballast, but booked for this on Sunday, 25 January, though only getting as far as Mossley when the motion came adrift and that was the end of her. No one considered repair worth the trouble. On 28 March both *5* and *55* had their last spoil working, the former then defying all prophecy by appearing on the 17.35 passenger to Whitehead on Easter Monday, her last day to haul any train. At this late stage *6* seemed to be trying to make up some lost ground with activity on the spoil trains, even as late as 23 April; but a fireman rushing off duty, neglected to fill her boiler and that was the end of her.

All in all, therefore, it seemed rather a case of necessity when it was announced that one train only (using two engines) would be on spoil train work for the last week, beginning 27 April. The previous day *4* had worked the steam crane to

Warrick's crossing, near Cookstown Junction, to assist, not
surprisingly, with a motorway bridge. This crossing was a few
yards away from overbridge 85, responsible in 1941 for the
death of Larne driver Sam Brown on the footplate of *73*, as
he looked back at his long goods train leaving the junction.
The final spoil working left Magheramorne with *53* at the
head and *4* banking, engine smokeboxes and one wagon having
a spectacular notice to the effect that 1,425,000 tons of spoil
had been transported during some 7,600 journeys.

The same afternoon both *4* and *53* were stabled in the old
shed at Carrickfergus. *4*, which had already worked local passenger trains on Easter Monday and Tuesday, was soon back
in use at York Road to assist *51* with a train of heavy girders,
and it was five months before she returned to Carrickfergus.
The scrap merchants soon dealt with *5, 6, 50* and *55* but it
was 1971 before *51* succumbed, to suit the accountants. Some
three months later, in July, an announcement of the pending
destruction of Carrickfergus shed seemed rather sudden, but
at least it did mean that after so much uncertainty the RPSI
was now the possessor of an NCC 2-6-4 tank (*4*). As she was
hauled to Whitehead the breakers were already at work
demolishing *53*.

Thus *4* will be the last of her class, just as the previous
NCC *4* was the last of class U1 to survive. Gratitude must be
expressed to those who organised this and those who contrib-
uted, so that another but more active NCC engine survives,
in addition to *Dunluce Castle.*

It is no great comfort to remind myself that the development of steam on many other railways has ended in the same
minor key, though apart from SR pacifics and a few Black
Fives in Lancashire the coda has seldom had the brilliance of
the NCC. Today's diesel drivers seem to find precious little
delight in their work, even if physically it is easier. I have
deliberately left a few NCC stories to the end to remind them
and you that amidst the dirt and discipline (and efficient
service) of steam days there was also more laughter and some
delight as well.

Despite the very contrasting accents of Belfast and Derry men the dominant NCC tongue has always had a Scottish flavour, be it the Larne, the Ballymena or the Coleraine variety. Scottish too is the name Malcolm, which crops up so often among NCC chiefs. Possibly the best known was Major Malcolm Speir, of whom a rumour, with a very NCC flavour, was that he would not have been averse to seeing his name on the birthday honours list, and that that was one reason why new engines *98-100* had received regal names. Certain it was that he demanded full attendance of his departmental chiefs on York Road platform in the eventuality of an important personage using the NCC. Top hats were regulation headgear on such occasions. On one such morning as he passed through, this lively general manager spotted a tell-tale hatbox and surprised everyone by scoring a splendid goal in the far corner of the room, whereupon the aggrieved owner of the 'topper' now stubbornly refused to wear it, quite spoiling the ultimate effect by appearing on the platform in a bowler.

A further example of an element of buffoonery in the make-up of this enterprising and now almost mythical man concerns the strange talents of a clerk called Fred Workman. This chap had a genius for imitating voices, but especially he could re-produce perfect signatures of all the NCC staff. On one hilarious occasion Speir arranged that a letter on locomotive department notepaper be typed out complaining that he (the manager) was interfering to excess in locomotive matters. Workman then signed Malcolm Patrick's name to the letter and the locomotive engineer was sent for. One can imagine the trend of the interview, with Patrick admitting that the signature was his but not the letter and the major hardly able to contain himself until his embarrassed subordinate had taken his bewildered departure.

Whilst the officers occasionally indulged in such frivolities, other ranks also had their moments of fun. I rather like the story of the driver who agreed to facilitate an ardent pigeon-owner by conveying a bird on the footplate from Coleraine to Antrim, where after noting the time he was to let it loose.

Whatever his original intent he could not in the end resist releasing the pigeon at Ballymena, nearly 12 miles earlier, though he still noted down his time at Antrim. When the hapless owner compared this with arrival time at his house he was so impressed that the bird was immediately entered for a big race, with disappointing results.

The humour here, if cruel, was deliberate. Just as often, however, it was unconscious and it was the onlookers who saw the funny side. There was, for instance, the Scrooge-like driver always on the lookout for overtime. Observed in conversation with a clergyman he was heard to say, 'I wouldn't mind your job. You are on every Sunday.'

There was also the driver who had listened at dawn to a midwife as she recounted the difficult circumstances surrounding the birth of a daughter to him. Eventually he said, 'You don't know what a bad night is. Now if you had to take sixty wagons up Ballyboyland bank!'

The youngest section of enginemen, the cleaners, also had their moments. During the blackout period of World War II the routine around midnight at Coleraine, when top-link driver Harry Molloy was bringing his engine in, was for someone to switch on the light at the turntable for such time as the mogul could be turned and stabled and the driver make his way home without falling into the pit. On one occasion, some few hours after the final act of this ceremony, the cleaners could see from their position up on one of the engines two figures approaching the shed and they realised that these were two policemen coming to complain about the bright lights. Just as the two 'coppers' entered the shed one of the lads managed to get to the master switch, thus turning out every light in the shed area. The boys could then listen to low mutterings and sudden blasphemies as the two investigators stumbled amongst the engines, for even in daylight it is often difficult to evade the hazards of typical shed furniture. In the end the policemen found their way out again and seemed only too glad to get away without solving the mystery. After all, the main purpose of their visit had now been accomplished. The light at the turntable was out.

The current campaign of violence by the IRA had affected the NCC very little until just a few days after I finished this book. Then Alec Eskdale could be seen on television describing severe damage to the parcels office and waiting room of his station at Waterside, Londonderry. Unpleasant as this has been, the effects on railway life cannot compare in tragedy with the results of the lack of government interest in the NCC since they took over responsibility for it in 1949. There is scarcely a mile of the route to Derry where the absence of a onetime station, junction, or siding does not constantly remind one of this.

Acknowledgements

So many sentences in this book have resulted from an unconscious remark from a railwayman which set me thinking and probing that it would be quite impossible now to name or remember all such sources, but I thank them all and especially those enginemen who have searched their memories and answered my questions.

A few outstanding enthusiasts must be named, starting with two locomotive inspectors of the NCC. Billy Hanley, though nearly ten years retired, is fortunately still with us and his successor, Frank Dunlop, has similarly, with an obvious love for his own railway, spared himself in nothing, even in matters far removed from rolling stock. It is an inspiration to listen to such men and in this category also is W. Steenson, shed foreman at York Road, who has shown tremendous enthusiasm that this book should appear.

Another NCC enthusiast is J.H. Houston of Whitehead, always willing to assist with vital information and well known for the care he has taken to preserve much of the railway which might otherwise have been lost.

Enthusiasm is almost an insufficient term for N.R.S. Foster of Dublin whose very frequent appearance on NCC trains during the past fifteen years tends to repudiate any idea that this railway, in its more standardised form, was less interesting. Mr Foster's logs, as well as some from earlier days by Andrew Donaldson and the late J.M. Robbins, help to fill a few gaps in my own experiences. R.N. Clements of Celbridge has also assisted in this respect, as well as offering valuable advice. Others, like him, have helped with photographs.